CREATIVE CONTROL

the secret to perfect innovation

brian w. bickford

ISBN-13: 978-1481805032

Book Cover by Kit Foster

Book Design & Layout by PIXEL eMarketing INC.

Legal Disclaimer

This book is dedicated to:

My wife, *Tatiana*, for being my creative muse and teaching me to trust in my own wisdom as a guide.

My son, *Maxim*, for being a living example for creating what you imagine and discovering the tools with unrelenting energy.

Knowledge Workers everywhere, who create, invent, and use the tools that allow for unlimited discoveries, education, and betterment.

Acknowledgments

Apart from my own efforts, the success of any project depends largely on the encouragement and guidance of many others. I take this opportunity to express my gratitude to the people who have been instrumental in the successful completion of this project.

I would like to show my greatest appreciation to those who took time to answer my many questions and allowed for confirmation of the solutions listed in this book. I cannot say thank you enough, and you know who you are, for this tremendous support and help.

It is the educators, businesses, partners, clients, investors, and people who engage in collaborations and contributions that make our world a better place to live in through their ingenuity and risks that I recognize fully as the catalyst for this book.

Contents

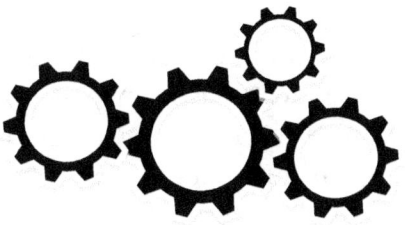

The Creative Process

*"I am always doing what I cannot do yet,
in order to learn how to do it."*

VAN GOGH

Let me ask you this: How many things have you created this year? Take a moment, think about it, and ask yourself what ideas, products, solutions, and events you played a part in. Whether they were on the job or not, take an inventory. What was the number? Does the number matter as much as the outcome? Which of those gave you the most pride and satisfaction?

Vincent Van Gogh also said, *"This creation-driven spirit is what forces us on above the limits of our imaginations. The creative 'process' makes us happy, productive, and honestly—brilliant."*

Through the years, I have enjoyed various levels of product innovation, either as creator or contributor. And each of those levels has numerous sublevels. Regardless, I loved every chance to create and collaborate, whether they were complex algorithmic data structures or hobby-oriented, such as sorting through several thousand outdoor photographs I take each year. The processes and outcomes can be similar. They can all begin with a great sense of possibilities and end in a high degree of satisfaction.

Much has been written on innovators, past and present. What we all want to know is what drives them to create. What is the "secret sauce" that brings them to game-changing innovation? Do you have the same capability and capacity to deliver something on the same scale as a Henry Ford, Bill Gates, Steve Jobs, or millions of lesser-known inventors?

I believe you do. I have seen it unleashed in the most unassuming locations within individuals and workplaces. Those moments are priceless.

Those who know me are aware that humor plays a large part in my communication style. Humor, when used for good, can relax, calm, and set the stage for fun. Fun can easily be turned into productivity; the free flow of ideas and the breakdown of the walls of anxiety and perceived expectations can refocus the group's or individual's attention to open-mindedness. With that, I have found there are many ways to unleash the potential for better problem solving, brainstorming, and ultimately, new innovation through the development of products, problems, and processes.

I have found that most people, myself included, are most productive and career-complete when we are creating something. To that regard, being attached to an endeavor in some critical or small way can lift one's ownership, thus increasing one's confidence in contributing to its ultimate delivery.

Have you ever worked or known someone who has worked at Google or Apple? They have a sense of complete ownership regardless of their position or distance from Silicon Valley. The secret for them may be the connection to something bigger than themselves or the perception that they are involved with a leading edge brand that is delivering adaptable and disruptive products. Regardless, pride and ownership are contagious. You feel it, and you want to be part of it. And you can!

Some people may get their creative outlet on the job, and others seek theirs in activities outside the workplace. I like the idea of integrating both. When a person can tap into that enthusiasm in any situation at any time, regardless of the environment, their contribution level skyrockets. One may ask, what does my love for downhill skiing have to do with the planning sessions at work? I immediately ask them what it feels like to ski on a perfect day. Tap into that emotion that allows you to open your senses and feel alive, confident, and brilliant. There are no negative adversities on that mountain or in that planning meeting. You know how you are going to negotiate that meeting like you would those black diamond trails.

I will challenge your senses in the chapters that follow, encourage you to question your reasons why you continue doing what seems like corporate culture or the path to least resistance, and push you to be open to learn what several others and I have done to bring creativity and innovation under control.

Together, we will look at different aspects of the planning process and ways to think about staff as a huge asset to your organization, determine where the plugs are, and create that environment for unlimited possibilities. It is the discovery of that one innovation or solution to a problem or reaching a collective pride in ownership that we look to achieve.

CHAPTER 1

Creative Control Theory

"Capital isn't so important in business. Experience isn't so important. You can get both these things. What is important is ideas. If you have ideas, you have the main asset you need, and there isn't any limit to what you can do with your business and your life."

HARVEY FIRESTONE

In general terms, creative control can be defined by how well a corporation, their teams, and individuals encourage involvement in the innovative process across their company. Who are the owners, gatekeepers, or moderators for new ideas in your company?

There is a complex mechanism at work here. Power, control, attitude, aptitude, agendas, introverts, extroverts, and pressure of deadlines and financial goals all have a say. Many times these attributes are observed and seldom addressed. Their impact usually suppresses the innovative spirit and leaves the visionary process to the same few. This, when observed, can be repeated over again due to perceived ownership. However, this does not have to be the case. These attributes can be used in favor of the creative process.

Some companies are great, with innovation and high spirits leaking from the ceilings. Then there are those suppressed "do your job" environments that choke the creativity right out of you. At these companies, you will find that there is a high rate of dissatisfaction, boredom, exhaustion, and turnover. I have a few theories that I'm going to share with you regarding the creative process.

Idea Generation in the Workplace

Imagine for a moment that one of your colleagues, the quiet one, the one who does not always "look the part" and sometimes may have communication issues, is the next Steve Jobs. What if we could get past the rough, or soft, exterior to get to his or her core contribution? This one employee could provide the output of several staff members and may have the likelihood of producing the next big thing. What if you gave everyone you work with that benefit? He or she may be completely unable to physically make those ideas happen, but the ideas themselves are great. Everyone in your organization is different, with various skills, talents, and levels of creativity.

We have more than 70,000 thoughts every day—I'm sure a few of them are wildly creative and perhaps even revolutionary. All innovation comes from the identification of opportunities or the creation of new ideas. None of this is possible without creative control.

So, if we have the capacity to generate tens of thousands of thoughts each day, how can we hone the quality of output to a time and place, generating on cue, when appropriate and without restraint? Will all ideas and innovations be brilliant? Most likely not! Success will lie in timing, dynamics, and ownership.

Knowing Your Stage – Timing, Dynamics and Ownership

Timing: It is a big day, and you are presenting to your board of directors. Conversations around financial performance are deep, and reasons for attributing factors are discussed with rapid-fire questioning. Board members state that the reasons for declines are tied to product lifecycle, and those customers are now interested in the new low-cost provider that has more value than what your company is offering. You recall a presentation you delivered a year ago that addressed that very situation and ways to offset the losses with new innovation. At that time, the board did not approve the costs for new product development.

Is now the time to represent that initiative? Probably not!

Now is the time to repackage and redevelop new teams in order to address a new economic system. You will use your team to define the new conditions, and you will brand your new initiative with a product name. Your new delivery to the board will be concise and to the point, using the brilliance developed from your new product development team. Now you have managed your timing on your conditions. Well done!

Dynamics: There is a new initiative that has an old sound to it. "Didn't we try this a few years ago?" Those are words that we hear a lot of in companies that have been around for five or more years. The new company should never hear those words, but they do come up from time to time. "I did that once, and it didn't work!" is the replacement.

Building your team is based on set up. You need to present your initiatives in the light of new and bright expectations in order to reset the dynamics of expectations. With the long string of people that will be involved in a project, communication will be the glue for driving that high, can-do energy.

Ownership: The boss is always right! Well...it is good to respect authority and it is good to be respected, but this dance can get sweeter if ownership lies wth the collective team. Agile, the process development method used in most programming departments these days, is about assigning ownership, usually to one person. However, like any good leader, they should be in the position of communicating with precision on behalf of stakeholders. Stakeholders will have ownership tied to their ability to express product characteristics and deadlines. Ownership for the milestones is with the delivery teams responsible for production.

Ownership should never be confused with controlling output, ideas, and contribution.

Idea Generation: One good idea is enough to make it big these days—either one or a collection of many consistently over a period of time. They cannot all be an Instagram, with a payout of a billion dollars. But we can work to advocate a climate of idea generation in the company. You are not just paying people to work; you are paying them to contribute, create, and add value.

Idea generation depends on four general things:

1. The average quality of ideas.
2. How many ideas are generated.
3. The variance of quality in the ideas.
4. Your ability to select the best ones.

The process sounds simple, but it is one of the hardest things to do as a manager.

This process relies on so many separate factors that introducing an idea-generation climate into a previously suppressed environment can be nearly impossible. People do not want to speak up. They fear their opinions. They fear not having any good ideas.

Begin your quest for creative control by releasing, allowing, and advocating for ideas that your employees have, and you'll be on your way. Don't stop this process—keep it going. You'll be amazed at the results after a few months if you reward people for their continued expression of ideas and creativity.

Creative Solutions to Unexpected Problems

Problem solving in itself is a creative process. Large or small issues all weigh and test our true resolve in applying creative principles that create action.

The financial crash of 2008 dramatically tested the business acumen of senior managers everywhere. For this book, I was given access to one of the leading Chief Marketing Officers in the world, who was called to apply and test his business acumen with urgency and persistence across a very large international organization. It was one of those situations that could have gone either way with implementing hard and surgical decisions.

David Norton, who then led Harrah's (now Caesars) Entertainment business during that critical time, knew the impact would require a very different approach in gaining consumer spending confidence and offsetting deep losses to the business. While the economy drastically impacted the customers' gaming behavior and revenue streams for the casino business, Harrah's needed to rapidly transform their process and organization dynamics.

To that regard, David's team deep dived the data and learned that the customers' demand curve had shifted down. They discovered that giving more offers and incentives was narrowing profitability. At a segment level, they needed to understand what programs were driving incremental profitability. He pushed for top-down, centrally-forced control groups to better understand the incremental process of marketing interventions and centralized marketing analysis to increase the speed and sophistication of insights that would be turned into the right actions with executive oversight.

David explains, *"We had analyzed revenue declines by micro segment, but it wasn't until we did direct research did we understand the customers' psyche. We discovered that our customers felt the experience wasn't what it used to be and that their expectations were even higher given gaming was more discretionary than in the past, especially for our best customers."*

Within a week, they formed a robust, cross-functional task force that analyzed the challenges in more detail and came up with several solutions. They further examined what customer service touch points mattered most to the overall experience and developed process and technical improvements to enhance the experience. They discovered customers who were assigned casino hosts and given direct care on a trip gave a much higher service score and had much better retention rates. As a result, David lowered the number of customers each host managed with the mandate and tools to touch all of their appointed customers.

David says, *"The real solution was in hiring true sales people to hunt for new revenue and creating a more robust sales culture, as well as providing near real-time data and training tools for our service teams to work with."*

"It was not an easy process," says David, explaining that each step took buy-in at every level of the cycle. *"The biggest challenge was convincing the organization that there was a need for change beyond the economic environment. The senior team knew we had to be surgical at a program and segment level. While moving quickly, the organization maintained tight control of the entire process, tested, analyzed, and then proceeded wider within a twelve-month period."*

Accordingly, evolving the team as you make significant operational changes to the marketing effort is as crucial as a "top-down" understanding of the process and potential effects to revenue. *"In moving to a more centralized process with the operators, our management presence was pentacle as we moved to a real-time interaction between customers and employees. Monitoring data from the Total Rewards loyalty program to develop the tools for our hosts to tailor value with customers greatly improved the conversion process."*

Besides improving revenue strategically and tactically, David attests that changing the team if they couldn't radically evolve with the times, while communicating the need to push innovation, makes the job more interesting and keeps "everyone focused on the adoption process." He further learned that there are many potential outcomes for which "the data" will help alleviate the potential "flaws in the implementation and those resistant to change."

So, What Is Creative Control?

Even in today's scientific community, no one knows conclusively how the neurological process works. Studies have been done and tests have been formed to unravel the science behind the computer of the human mind. To date, we can perform scans to indicate ideas of activity, but in no way is this useful in operating businesses today and getting the most out of your employees.

We know that creativity sets us apart as people and has put us on top of the food chain. Lions have teeth; we have creativity—as the analogy goes. But creative control, well, that's another problem altogether. How do managers learn to control something they can barely define?

There is one main reason why you are in business, and that reason is the same for your employees—financial performance and reward. Things such as freedom, creative expression, and other rewards are usually just bonuses in the job. What if you made these the focus of your business? What if creativity was something that could get you more rewards?

Creative control is thinking about things like this and then coming up with an actionable plan to motivate your teams and individuals to action with positive outcomes. David Norton's mind fired in the right sequences to address his dilemma, but

---

THE NETFLIX DECISION

Netflix has been one of the most successful dot-com ventures. In 2002 it was mailing about 200,000 DVD disks daily and went from 700,000 subscribers to nearly 15 million by 2010. In September 2011 Netflix announced its intentions to re-brand and re-structure its DVD home media rental service as an independent subsidiary company called Qwikster, totally separating DVD rentals and streaming. Andy Rendich, a 12-year veteran of Netflix, would have been the CEO of Qwikster. The new service would carry video games, whereas Netflix did not. However, in October 2011 Netflix announced that it would retain its DVD service under the name Netflix and would not, in fact, create Qwikster for that purpose.

Then, on October 24, 2011, Netflix announced it lost 800,000 U.S. subscribers in the third quarter of 2011 and more subscriber losses were expected in the fourth quarter of 2011. Despite the losses, earnings for Netflix jumped 63 percent for the third quarter of 2011.

Did this position hurt, hinder, or create value for Netflix? While a PR nightmare, the company posted a 2012 gain of 25 million subscribers. The course correction was an embarrassing tactic for the company, but they listened, learned, and continue their efforts to collaborate with content, distribution, and legal providers.

---

it was the entire team, top down, that resulted in a positive outcome.

I encourage daily questioning of the output, asking, "What have I created today? How have I made my company better? How can my creative contribution improve my job security? As an employer, how can I leverage the untapped resources of each staff member? How can I improve my hiring process to select only the best in adding to our creative value?"

Understanding What Is at Stake:

Understanding what is at stake is critical for those involved in the creative process, from the business model to the legal implications. Creative control lies in one's ability to think 360 degrees while understanding the wider implications.

While Netflix is a lesson on business strategy, it's also one about creative problem solving. It is the process of making bold moves, recognizing contingencies, and continuing on with product development on what was learned. These are things you will need to consider. Creative control means that you will be dealing with issues like these all the time.

Change and embracing change that comes from disruptive momentum, internal practices, and creative problem solving all manifests itself with the creative output spectrum. Creative control is about efficient management of intangible and often controversial concepts.

It is about learning how to be tactful in accepting one idea and turning others down. If you can get a team to work together, creating great ideas all the time, you have an unlimited earning potential.

In the technology industry, a good idea is pure gold. That's why you will need to learn how to handle these important points:

- Passion and loving what you do

- The ideas, opinions, and attitudes of your employees
- The amount of ideas and sorting them, choosing them, and testing them
- Deciding which teams go best together to get instant results
- Finding real creative talent, even if it's hidden in your company
- Giving back to your employees to keep them happy and fulfilled—the right reward structure to fit the situation

In other words, you need to leverage your own authority, influence, and creativity to get the best out of your teams and individuals at work. Instill the vision to allow your team to win, create, and innovate as they follow you to the ends of the earth. Only then will you finally be able to unleash the skill, power, and raw idea creation of these exceptional people. Be the kind of manager who encourages, explores, assists, teaches, inspires, and above all, leads by example.

In human history, there have been incredible innovators that have changed the way the world as we know it functions. We just have to remember Marie Curie, discoverer of radium; Alexander Graham Bell, the inventor of the telephone; and Carl Benz and Gottlieb Daimler, inventors of the car, to get a taste of what perfect innovation can do for a company and potentially a world changing event.

Today we have role models like Mark Zuckerberg, Facebook inventor; Steve Jobs, iPhone, iPad, and iPod inventor; and Fred Smith, founder of FedEx. These men implemented pure, ideal innovation in their companies with great success. Women driving business in today's economic climate—like Marrisa Mayer of Yahoo, former eBay chief Meg Whitman, and superstar CEO of PepsiCo, Indra Nooyi—are advancing innovation daily with the careful control of brand integrity, procedural methods, and financial performance expectations.

I've learned that to become one of these keen innovators means adopting a relentless search for perfect innovation. That means taking on a few characteristics that these great innovators were known for. They are influence, frame-shifting, seeing the interconnected system, mental time travel, and a disruptive mindset.

- *Influence:* If you do not have influence, you are just a dreamer. That is why great innovators are able to literally step into the hearts and minds of their target audience to gain their support. This is the opposite of what people usually do. Instead of reaching people on their level, we stay on the sidelines and try to lure people there—instead of simply walking over to their side in the first place.
- *Frame-Shifting:* If you can change your perspective, you can generate innovative ideas. It has been proven that innovators do this more often than the average person. Lose your keys and you will eventually run out of places to look—in the vase, on the tables, in your bedroom, on the key hanger. I bet if you had to drop to the floor, you would find them. It is a different perspective.
- *Seeing the Interconnected System:* Being able to see systems as a whole is a gift. Scipio Africanus did so when he defeated Hannibal—instead of facing the man head-on and losing, he cut off Hannibal's supply routes and disabled his entire system. If you can think in terms of seeing the interconnected system as a whole, your problem-solving skills will rapidly improve.
- *Mental Time Travel:* If you had to chat to a perfect innovator about their early career, you'd discover a mental time machine that works in perfect harmony, moving from then to now. Imagining future states is key if you're going to impact the world. The better you are at it, the more impact you'll have as a perfect innovator.

- *Disruptive mindset:* It is important to go after ideas that competitors will not pursue. It's how Google became Google and Sony went from making electric teapots to advanced smart electronics in a few short decades. Competition is key in business, and if you can do what they can't—or won't—then you are closer to being a perfect innovator.

The Active vs. Passive Work Environments

There are essentially two types of working environments, though these can vary according to company dynamics. In the technology field, it is extremely important to focus on having an active environment. High performance teams flourish within high performance companies. Once you decide you are first and foremost a company based on precision and passion, everyone will also believe that they are high performance innovators. This reduces barriers and increases expectations. Results will become self-governed and will run rampant.

When your company functions in a passive environment, your employees come to work, they sit down or stand (depending on what they do), and do it all day, without a second thought. They are not told that thinking, especially creative thinking, is something to be sought or rewarded.

We know the type that play safe and stick to their job descriptions—doing the bare minimum required to keep their job and to fly low under the radar. They are interested in survival and not contributions that look risky. They agree with the group and never rise above due to fear of exposure and being singled out as a risk-taker. Those days are gone. Companies cannot survive on "safe."

These people are very talented; they just have not changed with the times and conditions. That fear of risk is no longer of value. Letting this mindset prevail reduces job satisfaction. The number one reason for this is the lack of a creative outlet at work. Creativity leads to job satisfaction and an active working environment where employees can thrive, no matter what they do.

Active working environments are when managers allow the employees to become personally involved in the success of the business by making them care about it. They do this by focusing on utilizing their creativity at work. When people are creative and add something to a project, they care about it more.

This means that they put in extra effort, they work harder, and they constantly think of ways to make it better to get that outstanding result for the team. Funnily enough, this process was used to great effect in Ancient Greece, when individual minds used to obsess and philosophize over theories and ideas.

Then they would meet together in the senate and discuss all of these ideas at great length. The floor would be open to any senator who wanted to address the room. These men were never passive about their creative needs; they shared them openly and with anyone who would listen.

If you find that you have a passive working environment where there is just not enough social interaction, teams, or really the advocacy of creativity in your business, then you need to change that… now! For the good of your company!

An active business can be seen as a business with active minds that use the ideas from these minds to increase profits, extend reach, and promote themselves as leaders in the field. Without that, these days, you can't hope to last. Not in the tech field.

Why Collaboration Is the Key to Creativity

Solitude may be nice for painters, writers, and sculptors—but it is not the case in the technology environment. From the onset of conceptualization, there are many complex directions and processes that one must direct with a full host of contributors. If you can set the right conditions, the right people will emerge, elevating their game to engage in what I refer to as "artful innovation." This is when all pieces fall together and the collaboration group begins to hum. Everyone knows his or her roles, and leadership consistently encourages high performance. You will begin to feel and witness a new energy emerge. The stronger the team, the more dominant the creative environment becomes. Other groups replicate, and individuals become ambassadors for innovative progress.

There are several ways that you can improve the value of your collaboration techniques. These techniques were designed to bring out the best in your team and make for that perfect innovative cocktail that results in good ideas.

Keep in mind that collaboration is not about inviting different people to the same meeting, or the same people to different meetings, or, for that matter, working separately on the same project. You are meant to collaborate for communication, fun, team building, cross-disciplinary insight, and skills and to get more perspectives on one problem.

Your stakeholders and customers should be collaborative partners, because they are cogs in the creation process too. Collaborate with your peers and your project team and think outside of the box to find wildcard collaborators for additional perspective.

Much has been written on the subject of collaborative teams. It not only starts at the beginning of a project; it is a never-ending process. The larger the enterprise or more complex the business model is, the more numerous the members will be as part of the process. The derivatives can be numerous, with surprising and sometimes unexpected outcomes.

"The secret is to gang up on the problem,
rather than each other." - THOMAS STALLKAMP

In a company like yours, innovation is the ideal. It is the differentiation we are trying to establish, whether to a problem, a new product, or the company vision. The reason we seek perfect innovation is so we can outplay the competition. That is why we will need to focus on some rules for collaboration in creativity.

Rule 1: Create a collaborative expectation.

Start with developing the final outcome mission. This is the best way to help visualize the results. If you can visualize it, you can communicate it. This will surely alleviate any ambiguities on expectations.

Rule 2: Know your primary and secondary resources availabilities.

Product development can sometimes be very complex. The drivers—that is, those who will champion the process through the necessary channels—will be key. Allocation of resources and the time contributed to new or maintenance initiatives all impact the milestones. Identify contingencies and create for yourself the map for contingencies, if needed, while making time for course correction if needed. Your teams may discover some new issues, good or bad, along the way.

Rule 3: Everyone is part of the value chain.

There can be many perspectives involved in the process. Whether programmers, designers, coders, writers, legal, or financial, different perspectives provide more value to the final outcome. Changing the mix adds a different chemistry that might contribute brilliant ideas to your new project.

Rule 4: Advocate contribution.

Be open, hear what people say, share, and assimilate. Give feedback when it is expected and make your team members feel like their views matter. This is where setting the stage comes in. Everyone likes a bit of humor to lighten the tone. Set the vision with expected outcomes, deliveries, and milestones. Allow for input on critical issues. Time will always be a factor, and no one likes to spend their life in meetings.

THE GROUP GENIUS

There is a certain kind of genius that kicks in when you work with more than one person. I once had an employee work on a very difficult project, with a deadline in three days. It was just one of those times the board would not give us an extension. I gave full ownership to this lead project manager and went about my day. Before our due date, this very complex analysis was complete and perfect in every regard.

When I asked how she could have achieved such a thing, she said, "I assembled three other people in my department to assist me. They quartered the work and assembled one day ahead of schedule." Divide and conquer holds true. But so does trust!

I have learned from this example and others like it that you must trust in the accountability of individuals and teams you have established that when given the opportunity to succeed, they will.

Rule 5: Use communication tech tools.

Communication is key in maintaining collaborative engagements. Whatever your project management flavor is, use it and make sure others are familiar. When timelines and communications are disrupted, the project begins to fail.

Rule 6: Get to know your team.

If you know your teams well, you will know who goes well with whom and can better test these dynamics. Pairing people also helps the less courageous ones feel more comfortable if they feel supported. And likewise, I suggest taking walks each morning around the company to engage, interact and genuinely exhibit interests in all levels of the organization.

Rule 7: Establish a post-ops reflection.

At the end of each milestone, establish a post-ops review event. This is a time to learn from what worked or did not. I have found these extremely helpful in moving to the next phase of a project, and this keeps everyone collaborated with the initial vision.

Problems That Arise from Creative Control

There are many issues that you have to deal with once you seize control of the creative processes in your company. Here are a few to get you started:

- Corporate constraints. If you have some kind of management structure, corporate may not let you implement some creative solutions. The only way around this is to set up an open line of communication between your team and the senior team at the corporate level. Provide clear and concise initiative plans that outline its business logic and advantages using strategy, weaknesses, opportunities, and tactical approaches.

- No matter how hard you try, your development team may just not be able to achieve or reach the requirements or specifications laid out by management. In this case, you will have to refer to your contingency plan. If these perspectives have not covered this unique condition, gain contributions to the issue from your team.

- These conditions may influence the creativity-intensive process, leading to mistakes, a fall in morale, or a general lack of creativity because of all the red tape involved. A recalibration of the team to maintain their high performance and high energy will be in order. Most of the time individuals will act as professionals to solve the issues presented to them. If you made it this far, you can count on it that they will solve new conditions.

- There are many approval processes that come up in the tech world—constantly it seems sometimes—and you have to pass them all. You won't pass them all though, and there will be back and forth changes on occasion. Implement an iron-clad process to speed up approvals, like using the popular Agile development method.

- There is always a risk that product reallocation can occur at the senior level, thus diverting talent and resources. While rare, these situations do occur. Regardless of new awareness or corporate shifts, be prepared.

- Fight for your projects and defend resource allocations (who gets what development time and by who). Not all programmers, creative talent, and business managers are created equal. Regardless of team players, be prepared to set the stage, defend vision, and monitor output.

- Group communication can break down, leading to disputes about projects and other things. That is when you need to step in and sort them out before your team

THE MIGRATION TO AGILE

Even today, companies are migrating to processes that are seemingly new to them but have been the standard for others for a while. I have seen Agile be introduced to small and large enterprises on several occasions. This can sometimes take over a year to change the product programming culture from a waterfall approach to Agile.

There is usually some resistance and slowing of the process until fully and widely accepted. I have also seen where resistance to change resulted in a hybrid methodology that only that organization could understand, thus defying the purpose of an interchangeable process. Senior support, clear objectives, and deadlines for adaptability could have fixed these situations.

disintegrates. People will take sides, and you will lose your best team.

- You always have problems with customer satisfaction, mitigating creative risk, and, of course, the entire creative process performance.

With every problem, there is a solution. Remain upbeat, keep your staff and teams focused on the vision, and know your course correction and recalibration plan. The final result is that the entire company will benefit. Remember the Google effect? You want your staff and overall company to shine with pride. Everything else can be overcome if your team is focused and dedicated.

THE BULLY FACTOR

When I took over the management of the product development team of a tech company a few years ago, a culture of bullies existed, particularly toward the product manager team. Once I identified the culprits and removed them, a few employees became product development superstars. There was one in particular who went on to lead some of the largest commercial e-commerce properties in the world.

Bullies are like graffiti; they erode value and prevent the true value of an asset. Recognize the dynamic of your teams and control the prevalence of negative influences quickly.

Learning to Control the Innovative Environment

The opportunities to create something special are few, unless you are the type who can find innovation in everything you do. That is the type of people we all want to be around. If you start your day with the attitude that you can make a difference, ultimately you will make a difference. You will attract top level talent to your company as the word spreads that you are a company working on innovative projects; that you have top talent to work with, learn from, and share; and the environment is one that is open to new ideas.

Most individuals who choose the technology career path are all those things and more. They are already enthusiastic and ready to take on new challenges. It is up to a keen sense for managing the innovative environment that will separate one company from another. Which one are you? If you are reading this book, you are of the breed of management that wishes to get the best out of their company.

While most are smart collaborators interested in showcasing their talents, there are others that can degrade the process. They may in fact believe they are contributing to excellence as they see themselves as the smartest or most valuable. These are not bad attributes, but they can become toxic. The ultimate goal with learning how to control the creative environment is empowerment. Even though having power is seen as a bad thing in many businesses (because of bullying and abuse), it is actually a very liberating thing. It is also an opportunity to NOT be that person and to use your power for good—in a wholesome, creative way.

Control is about power. But creativity is intangible. You cannot force creative people to be creative or try and trick them into doing what you want. None of those things work if you want your business to change from a passive to an active model.

You need to use your creative power to inspire creative empowerment in others so that they can also inspire it in their teams! It is a never-ending cycle of empowerment, and it results in confident, proud, caring people that love what they do at work. That's exactly what you want.

Understand these core concepts in business, and you are on your way:

- While business is about beating your competitor, providing quality and prosperity for all involved, it is also about the emotional condition of the enterprise. Once you create an open culture where one can tap into their creative sides and express their potential, you will immediately see more value for high performance output of every employee on your team
- Advocate a cooperative and learning environment where fact-based evidence is useful as a tool and for aligning conditions and expectations. With consistency, your

teams will emulate what is given to them. Excellence will beget excellence, and pride will turn into collaboration.

- Do not forget to be inspiring, motivating, and strong. Paint positive images of things wherever you go, and be the leader that creative people need. Be strong, tall, and motivating—and show them how much they can accomplish if they become the creative people that they are.

Control your creative environment by unleashing creativity in the workplace:

- **Motivation:** Learn what drives and motivates people. Think about what motivates you. Is it money, position, power, or control? It is for most people. Creative Control is about giving people what they want most...control. When you identify that and apply it to the principles of your environment, you can unleash an individual's condition to collaborate and contribute.

- **Measure Contribution:** Learn from your peers and staff on how they contribute and when. If they are only in triage mode, and that is what gets them going, learn and acknowledge how they can produce more in other situations. Not all events are or have to be outwardly on fire. Use the fire within to contribute to even the most mundane issues.

- **Understand Reward:** Some people are fulfilled when they write the perfect, bug-free code. Others feel appreciated when listened to. We are aware of all the reward triggers that encourage performance and create the environment for innovation, and I hope that just working in your awesome company will be reward enough. That is what we are trying to create. This is not as tangible as money, but a happy, creative workplace increases retention and fulfillment.

INSPIRING WITH A YOUTUBE VIDEO

Most everyone has seen the cute squirrel on water skis. This is an endearing visual. Occasionally, to break things up, I ask one or two people to bring a YouTube clip of something that inspires them. Some have shown compelling sports feats, some have provided clips of an unselfish act of kindness, and I have seen others present clips of the humorous side of the tech industry. These are silly, but it puts everyone at ease.

I guarantee that your meeting will have an open, active result if you allow one or two people to show a video of what inspires them to open the meeting.

- **Tools:** Make sure you are giving your staff the right tools, within reason. We all like new and shiny. Make sure the tools fit the situation. That is the investment needed to inspire a rich environment and help make people feel understood. However, the perceived lack of resources should not limit one's contribution; mostly due to the fact that, "If my budget was bigger, I could do x or z." And this is a black hole for productivity. You must create the vision that they can conquer the world with only a toothpick. Within reason, the lesson is learned.

CHAPTER 2

Creative Ideology 101

"It's easy to come up with new ideas; the hard part is letting go of what worked for you two years ago, but will soon be out of date."

ROGER VON OECH

My ideology is based on personal experience and wisdom developed from practicing better management outcomes. With that, I believe that corporate management is responsible for leveraging the talents of its employees. How should I best leverage the human asset? Unleashing the creative spirit of course!

Combine creative energy with thoughts, talent, and ideas, and the world is your oyster. The first person is hired, trained, and molded into a student of creativity.

There is a lot to consider when it comes to building an environment that is different from what people are used to. Behaviors for individuals and groups are as similar as they are dissimilar. I know that may sound contradictory, but it is hard to say that all situations and corporate environments are the same. That is, some strategies will work brilliantly some of the time and some will work all the time, and other times they do not fit at all. The complex human, and your fellow work colleagues, all want to conform and fit in, but there are multiple dynamics at work here. How do I get everyone to play nice and conform to a way of thought or process?

Most resistance to change is centered on fear and anxiety. We have all heard that fear of failure is a motivator. But that course of behavior is not always the perfect outcome. No one wants to feel incompetent, look dumb, be wrong, or be judged. A lot of risk is associated with speaking out or stamping your name on a new project or initiative. Avoiding risk is a normal human trait. Danger, stay away! In perfect groups where you are paid to be brilliant every day, in every meeting, there is a lot of risk.

Guarding is a term used in the medical profession for when a patient is injured and they tend to direct you away from the pain center. A fighter will put their left foot in front to protect their right side injury. You will notice that guarding is also something that an individual will do because of some prior experience. You need to recognize that once you remove the fear and anxiety factors from the individual or group environment, they can use that energy for more productive activities.

In the last chapter, we discussed briefly the importance of understanding drive and reward. What drives you may not be what drives me. However, collectively, if we are both focused on the same outcome with the same rules, our drive becomes synergistic. Here we revealed the effects of risk and anxiety.

With those significant traits being identified, we now can get started with controlling and lifting the creative factors that make great innovators.

So what makes an individual creative? I believe it begins with just getting started. Once you walk into that meeting or take on any initiative, you have started the creative process. So when do you begin to innovate? That also began when you started. Innovation is a derivative of participation. Solving problems and finding the best solution with the conditions you are working on sets the stage for a free flow of ideas and outcomes.

I have found that setting the stage for myself with a few positive statements, said silently to myself, puts me in the right frame of mind that will ultimately transcend to others around me.

Pre-meeting Mantra

> *"I acknowledge that I am in control of my creative input and that I will contribute without anxiety or restrain. I look at my peers' ideas as brilliant and having the potential to solve our dilemmas. I wish to support and compound their input with mine. Together we will both succeed, and our group will impress the company as a whole. Other groups in our company are also brilliant and willing to engage each other to make it stronger."*

We want each and every group to become that crack-team of creativity and innovation. Once we believe that our own efforts have value, the core of our groups and company will begin to take shape as the company you always wanted to work for.

Working with Group Creative Processes

About one hundred years ago (1913) the greatest invention was the first modern brassiere that received a patent to New

York socialite, Mary Phelps Jacob. That same year Ecstasy, the parachute, windshield wipers as the standard on all cars, crossword puzzles, and mass production at the Henry Ford factory in Highland Park, Michigan, were invented. Look around yourself now and see how sustaining some processes and products are and how they have been sustained in today's world.

Depending on where you work and the career you have selected for yourself, there are numerous ways that you and your company could think of that would offer a lower cost alternative through more efficient ways to produce. Those ideas could be priceless, but left hidden, they help no one.

The Chinese invented toilet paper[1] in 50 BC (thank you, by the way), and it was not until the early 1800s that Thomas Crapper purchased the "Silent Valveless Water Preventer" patent and later brought it to the masses as the modern day toilet. The years between observing the need, identifying a solution, and fulfilling the need on a mass scale were multiple. Credit is rarely given to Albert Gilblin, who worked for Thomas Crapper. If so, we would have had a different slang word for this great invention.

With information technologies, we are now working at a much faster pace with higher expectations on turnaround times. Every day I work in several different countries dealing with multiple unrelated groups building some of the most interesting programming solutions and solving dilemmas. Some groups we self-select, but for most cases, our teams are handed to us and we migrate through, sometimes with ease and other times facing complications. It is how we deal with the adversity that makes us great creators and innovators.

Some of the simpler solutions can have dramatic effects

---

1   Who invented the toilet?, toiletpaperworld/blog. http://blog.toiletpaperworld. com/who-invented-the-toilet/

on a company. Creativity simply is an interesting tactic when it comes to assessing the environmental economic system to see what might work even when profits are up and goals are being met. These may be assets and resources owned internally, or they may exist within the business category. Take, for instance, a company like TripAdvisor and what it has done to make business transparency part of the travel industry. Small boutique hotels to large multi-branded chains now are dependent on the TripAdvisor process.

Acquiring hotel bookings is a very competitive prospect, challenged with the right mixture of loyalty enticements in order to reduce guests' choices to a single hotel brand or two. Getting consumers to filter down to the location, cost, and hotel is a marketing dilemma that takes the keen understanding of consumer behavior and business acumen. Statistically, "lookers become bookers" only after consulting eight different hotel accommodations online, says one study. I know that I only book when the reviews average 4 or 5 ratings on TripAdvisor.

There is one person I want to introduce you to who I have met several times and think of her as the face of productivity. Dynamic and able, Robin Korman, Senior Vice President of Global Loyalty at Wyndham Hotel Group, is faced with business dilemmas and numerous internal and external challenges on a daily basis. As the overseer of the largest hotel loyalty program with 14 brands and 7,000+ locations, Robin navigates keenly between managing highly elastic consumer demand and communication with franchised owners and senior management teams that have high expectations on the performance of loyalty rewards members. The Wyndham Reward program is the gateway for data assimilation and decision-making at various levels of the organization.

According to Robin, who started overseeing Wyndham Rewards in 2009 after nearly six years managing the global loyalty program at Starwood Hotels & Resorts, it was part of a new management wave. Several new hires at senior levels within the company helped open the pipeline for innovations and business processes. Previously, Korman states, *"When things are working well, the appetite for risk is low. However, we saw the world was changing; travelers were able to access so much more customer-generated content on places to stay, and the online travel aggregators were becoming such a big and expensive part of our business that we knew we had to change without risking a decline in performance."* Wyndham Hotel Group is faced with the same perplexing business issues other consumer-centric industries continually struggle with: economic conditions, a rapidly changing competitive landscape, product substitution, and price sensitivity.

A recent victory for adaptable change at Wyndham Hotel Group was the introduction of TripAdvisor.com user ratings next to each property description on the branded websites that allow travelers to sort the hotels in a destination by rating. Since 87% of travelers consult TripAdvisor prior to booking or 53% of respondents would not book a hotel that does not have reviews on its site, the Hotel Group wanted to make it quick and simple for travelers to access the information and keep them on the Wyndham Hotel Group sites rather than risk losing them once they went to TripAdvisor to check reviews.

The TripAdvisor reviews were initially placed on the Wyndham Rewards loyalty website. As a result of the careful assessment and collaboration across the organization, including brand operations, IT, and e-commerce to implement the ratings system, the company immediately experienced a 30% increase in bookings and rolled the ratings out to all 14 brand websites. According to Robin Korman, this could not have been achieved if it were not for the top-down presence of management involvement in removing the threat of change. *"Many people voiced their opinion about the implications of placing unfiltered comments on our branded websites. We implemented the ratings along with extensive training to show our franchisees how to respond to the customer feedback posted there. We knew that close monitoring of the data would be warranted with regular management reporting if we were to leverage the ratings to our advantage."*

This was a bold move by the Wyndham Hotel Group team as the initiative expanded to all 14 brands after only three months of testing. Today, the company continues experimenting with cross-collaborative teams in a measured and calculating way, which may not have been the case three to four years prior.

While a seemingly simple solution to a problem in any form, the contribution and collaboration needs the right combination of control, communication, and commitment. This is what I believe is the winning formula.

Group collaboration is critical for team buy-in and continuity throughout a course of action for driving new initiatives.

When engaging the group, members and individuals have a responsibility to be effective as a creative unit:

- **Awareness** – Preparation is expected with a useful perspective on the issues being discussed.
- **Time** – Be as efficient as possible and respectful of those involved. Use meetings to gain clarity, consensus, and solutions.
- **Values** – Stay true to your professionalism. Understand the corporate values and overall project mission.
- **Evaluate** – Call into question your own contribution. Ask yourself if you have met the other attributes above.

My creative ideology is always that group creative processes were the best and the most difficult to perfect. Several minds are definitely better than one when it comes to working on creative projects in the information technology industry.

FINANCIAL COMFORT ZONE

Many people have heard me say more than once that "it is always fun building things. The hard part is making money." I caution teams to be keenly aware of the potential return on investment on each of their activities. Pressure on financial performance can be felt even before an initiative begins, and this can disrupt the development process if due diligence is not conducted in advance of development resources. You will save your time, your team's resources, and potentially your job if you know how to defend activities as they relate to R&D.

Creative Ideology in Teams

Why aren't groups creative? You get teams in all businesses, and yet so few of them have the capacity to perform in a creative way. Yes, individuals can perform, but there are so many stumbling blocks for teams.

They need to reject these "norm" ideologies and adopt the creative process ideologies instead. Let's take a look at the difference here.

Normal Group Ideology

Lack of collaboration and high competition among group members, which is the "old school," get ahead mentality, discourages creativity in the workplace. Team members make themselves look good instead of sharing and collaborating. Restructure the way you run your groups, and invite equality, collaboration, and open innovation into your teams. No individual is allowed to dominate a single meeting.

WHAT IS 80/20 ITO?

The ITO (Innovation Time Out) policy encourages Google employees to spend 80% of their time on core projects and roughly 20% (or one day per week) on "innovation" activities that speak to their personal interests and passions.

- Conformity has always stifled creativity, but this particular kind makes it hard for individuals to talk to each other. There must be a manager or leader talking, and there are many rules to follow or you will get into trouble.
  - *Solution:* Encourage non-conformity and risk-taking and don't punish those that break away from the herd while brainstorming. Creativity and innovation need to be supported by a group leader.

- Communication differences lead to clashes or dysfunction. Some are loud and outspoken, others shy and introverted, some are disinterested or rude, and others are irritating. In these meetings, only one or two people are heard.
  - *Solution:* Equal communication must be encouraged by allowing each team member to present or talk about their ideas during a meeting. Every concept needs to be examined and explored.

- Cultural norms, where only a set group of people are allowed in the group, limit the amount of diversity and perspective a group can achieve. The world is seen in one way and one way only.
  - *Solution:* Choose team members from different departments, or who have unique perspectives on a project. Adding an accountant to a team, for example, may lead to more cost-effective project solutions.

- Sneaky, get ahead play is where all communication is defensive in an old school team. You want to be the best, so you hide information and sabotage other people's efforts. You aren't honest, and you are only out for yourself.
  - *Solution:* The team needs to understand that they succeed as a whole and should work together as one unit too. When the project gets ahead, everyone benefits, not just a single team member. It's time to broaden the way you reward your teams.

Creative Group Processes

- *Supportive communication means that no one is judged, accused, or able to get ahead by not sharing information.* Everything is out there because the IDEA is the most important part of the meeting, not following meeting rules.
- *All inventive, innovative creativity is rewarded in one way or another.* Whether it's just clapping, saying, "That was great,'" or getting a bonus—you are appreciated, individually and as a team.
- *Collaboration, whether you like it or not, makes things faster and better.* It's like comparing a dictatorship to a democracy. The democracy is always going to be the one that wins.
- *Be and teach your creative types to be active listeners.* Instead of just waiting your turn to speak, take notes and say what you need to say at the end. Everyone must be heard properly for an accurate creative decision to be made.
- *Be innovative but firm, and set a routine for your creative staff.* They will work well together if they are monitored. Leave them alone too long and tomfoolery could result with very little work being done at all.

Using Vision to Inspire Creativity

Vision defined means "something seen in a dream, trance, a thought or concept, or something seen in the imagination." Does this sound familiar? Most creative processes start off as visions. When you sit in a group creative process, you realize that visions come on thick and fast, and your imagination goes wild.

That's because one person's vision can spark ideas of your own. Vision should be used in group sessions to inspire the rest of the group to come up with their own special ideas or idea add-ons that will help the project.

What I like to do is present the concept of "inverted funnel." While most planning sessions focus on big picture to small supportive elements, Inverted Funnel begins with the smaller element, building off those as blocks to a larger vision. The theory is based on the fact that, with core solutions, we can begin to understand the larger implications to solving issues or developing a new source of income.

VISION INSPIRES LEADERSHIP

As the leader of your group of creative minds, it's your job to instill vision in what they do. Ask lots of "user" questions, such as:

1. Who is the customer?
2. How would this work?
3. What is different about this solution?
4. What resources do we currently have that could add efficiencies to this solution?
5. What would be the opposite to doing this?

Leader questions serve as a means to flushing out other perspectives.

Using Perception to Inspire Creativity

Perception is defined as "the ability to hear, see, or become aware of something through the senses. It's also a state of being or process of becoming aware of something in a certain way." Some people call perception "understanding"—which is important for creativity.

There are so many things that inspire creativity, but if you do not have the right perception of them, you will miss the beauty completely. Everyone perceives the world differently. This is why some people like the color pink, while others hate it.

So creativity is subjective in art, but not so much in business. In business, you can use perception to inspire creativity in your teams. How you ask? Like this...get them to:

- Understand the project on an intimate level, have them talk about it, and begin to throw around ideas about it. When they know the project and the clients, they'll better understand what is required of them.
- Recognize the talents in each other. Help them spend enough time together so that they learn about each other's strengths and weaknesses. That way, when a project happens, the team will know how to split the resources.
- Understand the business and what you want from them. While you abide by the creative process, you are still part of a business and exist to make money. That means that you have the final say. It also means that your staff members need to love your creativity and know you as a leader.
- Understand the other teams in your business. There will be times when you have to collaborate, and they may have a completely different creative process than you do. If they know that in advance, they can work on it and compromise, and things will turn out better.

Perception is about the problem and what solution best accomplishes a profitable result. Perceive what the client wants from the very beginning, and you have a winner. If management wants an Android app in blue that tracks people when they run, do not give them one in reds, greens, and yellows—give them a range of blues to choose from. That is just common sense and stays in the framework of the problem and solution.

Your team will need daily inspiration and understanding; and even though perception is not something you can always get right, it is something you can continually practice.

Learn to be open-minded and perceive things differently through the eyes of your stakeholders, co-workers, team members, and company.

It can be hard to continually remain creatively inspired. But perception is part of the curiosity gene that makes people so good at being creative. Without perception, everything you learn would make no sense. You always need an angle or a direction. Just keep in mind that yours isn't always the only one!

Using Collaboration to Inspire Creativity

The best forms of creativity are not as we previously thought—the genius work done by loners—but the work done by collaborations of people pitching in to create something special. Did you know that COINS exist in the world, or Collaborative Innovation Networks, where online communities of people work together to create innovations?

Entire communities of orthopedic surgeons swap ideas on how to treat spinal injuries for example. Now that's collaboration!

THE STATS DON'T LIE

According to the *Creative Research Journal,* an individual's creative output is directly related to the social environment. Put them with a team of people they like and enjoy working with, and you'll get maximum productivity. Put them with people they don't like, and no ideas leave their lips.

Creative processes are facilitated by the physical environment, which is why choosing your teams is so important. I have had a mismatched team, and they nearly tore each other apart—just because there was one person the other team members did not like!

Design and User Experience in Collaboration

There is real value in user experience. You need to work on things that matter to your company and to the world. Everyone has experiences—from your consumers, employees, and competitors to your customers. How do these experiences affect the outcome of a project?

Experience itself is simple, subjective, emotional, physical, and something you remember or learn a valuable lesson from. Every product has a user experience that touches people in different ways. Two people could be brought into a room and given an iPod. One will love it, because all they used before was a CD player. The other person will hate it, for a personal reason. The other may hate it because they will have to digitize all their CD music library to the new digital format.

A great product is about the big picture and the small details that make up a perfect user experience. If you can make people enjoy your product, you're already successful. It is your team's job to design user experiences.

Experience design involves HOW you create a product. That's why it works better when teams do it. When there is more than one person working on experience design, more people will end up liking that product because of the different perspectives and ideas that have gone into it.

Consider the lifecycle of a product before you begin creating it. How do you react to similar products? Did the intended experience come across, or did it fall short? Every user experience is an interaction with your company.

Create user experience polls to quantify your intended results. Products should be good looking, simple to use, pleasant, interesting and fun. Finally, get the right people to use your product so that it is guaranteed to be successful. A good reputation is everything.

Be the first choice, the most affordable choice—or at least have a very good reason to be a little more expensive than other products. Products that are the most successful are the ones that everyone simply must have. Without your product, they would fall behind in technology or miss out on a huge trend.

There's more competition than ever before; people can get what you make in Asia for next to nothing. Only real innovation and exclusivity is going to get your company where it needs to be. There is no such thing as a "good enough" user experience—it has to be PERFECT. That's what you're striving for with your creative teams.

Here's how to use creative collaboration to inspire creativity:

- Different voices have different perspectives, which lead to the examination of decisions on a micro level and better decision making overall.
- The more ideas you have, the more chance your team has of impressing your clients or blowing them away with something really special.

- Honing in on that one good idea is worth the group collaboration, and it will inspire your team to greater heights when everyone loves it.
- You have your own special think tank where ideas can be created, examined, and used or discarded. That's something great for a creative company.
- Bringing in a new person or a new project evokes change, which reenergizes everyone and leads to mass inspiration all over again.
- Focus, chat, decide, act—that's what collaboration is all about. It works like a charm for your creative team.
- Collaboration helps you stay on track and focus on your part of the work so that you don't let your team down.

Collaboration will always inspire creativity because creative spirits feed off each other. Put them all in a room together with a purpose, teach them some basic skills—and you will soon have an unstoppable force that can take on any job and perform any miracle!

Reward and Creative Fulfillment

There are many myths that go around about creativity and how you should promote it in the workplace. When I talk about rewards and fulfillment, I'm referring to the base needs of all creative people. And because all people are creative—we all need these things!

Creativity, while it can be motivated by money, does not come from money. According to Harvard Business School research[2] on money, people don't think about their salary on a day-to-day basis. What they do think about is how they FEEL

2   Breen, Bill. The 6 Myths of Creativity, http://www.fastcompany.com/51559/6-myths-creativity

while they are working. Are they bored? Tired? Listless? Unchallenged? Frustrated? Angry? Sad?

Emotions play a huge role in the daily activities of your employees. Surprisingly enough, emotions are also at the core of creativity. In fact, many creative geniuses of our century were known to be completely emotionally unstable. Einstein, for example, regularly saw a therapist and couldn't perform simple tasks such as brushing his own hair.

Emotion is strongly connected with the reward and creative fulfillment need in your employees. This is not going to improve by adding heavy time deadlines to your work either.

The same study showed that creativity rapidly declined when people were rushed or made to meet a deadline. Creativity is best explored in relaxing, calm, and almost "thoughtless" environments. Daydreaming, for example, has been found to produce great creative ideas in people who felt creatively drained or blocked.

It is my firm belief or ideology that teaching skills such as new visualization, changing perceptions, and collaboration in teams produces the best possible results. Concepts such as "don't try to force creative thinking" and "don't bribe creativity out of people" work. Here are a few more I think are very relevant if you're going to gain creative control.

- Creativity does not just come from artists, illustrators, and writers only. These stereotypical creative types may be great at design and horrible at coming up with fresh, lucrative ideas for your business. Everyone has the potential to become a superior innovator once they realized their potential.
- Using fear and despair to motivate creativity out of your employees is like using massive budget cuts and triple shifts to inspire your employees. Creativity is associated with love, joy, happiness, excitement, and passion—not

anxiety, fear, and sadness. You'll only ruin your chances of getting any good ideas out of them.

- Being competitive in any working environment may be an old mantra that works, but it doesn't work so well, according to the Harvard Study, if you're looking to unleash and improve creative thinking. Instead of competition, where you pit one creative against another, or worse—teams against each other—promote collaboration for better results. This is non-threatening and will work like a charm.

If you want your employees to feel that deep sense of creative fulfillment, then allow them to be part of the success of the project. Do not bribe, trick, disrespect, or slave-drive your creative staff. In the tech field, they will be brilliant in their own time (within reason).

CHAPTER 3

Creative Influencers in Business

"Imagination is not only the uniquely human capacity to envision that which is not, and, therefore, the foundation of all invention and innovation. In its arguably most transformative and revelatory capacity, it is the power that enables us to empathize with humans whose experiences we have never shared."

J.K. ROWLING

There are many creative influencers in business—you just need to know where to find them! Diversity in business is one of the most incredible things in the world of creativity and change. No two people experience the world the same way, and so there is never a shortage of ideas, cultures, or adventures to draw upon.

These creative influencers must be found within your business and nurtured. These skills can be improved and strengthened with the right company that has the ability to develop its' employee's strengths. Together, with a team of striking creative individuals, you can change the direction of your business.

The Corporate Petri Dish

The corporate Petri dish is much like a family. It contains different types of people who like different types of things. There are personality differences, social dynamics, social clashes, norms, rules, and rebellions. All in all, your corporate Petri dish IS a FAMILY.

Businesses, unfortunately, do not treat their employees like family members. What could a junior coder possibly know about creating a fix for an extremely complex piece of software? A lot, actually, if you listen to them. The old conventions are gone. It's not experience that counts anymore; it's creativity.

Albert Einstein once said, *"Imagination is more important than knowledge."* To that point, any person has the ability to contribute and influence, regardless of age, levels of acquired wisdom, and experience. Everyone has the capacity to express and the desire to share their perspective. The shared experience that comes from exchanging ideas is powerful.

In a Petri dish, with the lid on, some personalities thrive and others fail. There is a wide spectrum of people that are able to contribute to the conversation and others that don't say anything at all. Some still have all the great ideas, while there are others that will tell individuals about their ideas later. Everyone is different.

Who are the people who give the talkers the ideas? Where do they come from? How can we get them to become leaders in your business? Visionaries may start out shy, but they are born to lead people—even if the vision isn't totally clear at the time.

Most of all, how do these ideas ever become actions, if we're not actively searching for our creative influencers? Who really owns a concept, and who just takes the credit for it? These are all issues that will arise while you advocate creative expression at work.

The moment the job description is down on paper, the expectations for your employee's job are set. There will always be benchmarks or baseline features that are included that help your employees do their jobs as prescribed.

But job descriptions are flawed. They say nothing about the conditions you'll be working in, the personalities you will connect with or be repelled by, or the many obstacles you'll face. They just don't ask you to be what the business needs you to be: passionate, creative, inspiring, and excited about the work that you do.

Thriving or Surviving with Creativity

The key to creativity is not only finding out that the individuals in your company should be collaborating together—it's that you need to be examining each of these people in order to find the creative influencers.

Programmers define the design process as a recursive function. The power of recursion evidently lies in the possibility of defining an infinite set of objects by a finite statement. In the same manner, a finite recursive program can describe an infinite number of computations, even if this program contains no explicit repetitions. Simply put, once a goal is established, the creative process involves a sequence of development techniques, sometimes through the process of elimination, that help clear the path to defining, developing, and deploying the solution. An influencer has an innate understanding of the flow to information, information processes, and sorting solutions.

Thriving with creativity means giving more voice and responsibility to the creative influencers than to the doers. These are the people who will help you generate enough exceptional ideas that your doers can then take, think about, change, and create. Thinkers may not be doers. You might occasionally get an inventor—or a thinker and a doer—but they are rare.

Years of personal experience have taught me that if you don't sort out the creative influencers from the doers, you could run into a lot of trouble. I know I've said that everyone is creative and that they ALL deserve a voice. But I also said it's up to you to choose which ideas are the most worthy of becoming tangible things.

The best ideas are appropriate, actionable, and useful. They have a beginning, a middle, and an end. More to the point, they have a very good reason for existing. If you don't want to simply survive in a creative environment, which, believe me, can get very rowdy and out of hand at times, then you'll need a way of identifying the creative influencers.

Creative thinking is about how someone approaches a situation just as much as it is about why, when, or any other reason.

The Implications of the Creative Process

How do you spot a creative influencer you may ask? One of my graduate professors used to say, "What would Bill Gates do?" as a means to lifting one's innovative potential in a humorous way. There are steps that you need to take and traits that you need to watch out for in order to locate, perhaps promote, or at least segregate these gems from the rest. These are the implications of the creative process before they have begun.

Keep in mind that creativity is how you approach things, how you react or act in certain situations, how you perceive things, and, naturally, your curiosity levels and courage.

#1: Curiosity

All highly creative people are genuinely, maddeningly curious. They are great media consumers; they love to ask questions, and when they don't know something, they generally find out the answer…usually on Google.

#2: Courage

Creative influencers are courageous in that they are not afraid to take creative risks or to share these ideas with people that may shun them. A rough, silly idea may become the best idea you've ever heard if you just listen out for it.

WHAT I'VE FOUND ABOUT CREATIVE BUSINESSES

I've worked with many companies, both creative and not so innovative. Creative companies tend to not repeat themselves in projects so much and get a great reputation for original, innovative thinking. They also have high value added processes and are knowledge-intensive.

Creative companies approach creativity from all angles, which means everyone is creative, so there is a high level of flexibility, adaptability, and openness to change. Creative risks are often rewarded with enormous returns and even better bonuses for the people involved. All in all, the creative process should be your business process.

#3: Expressive

Many creative types can't help but be themselves. They feel drawn to individuality and reject the ideas of other people. They are also able to tell you exactly what their ideas are and where they came from. These expressive folks love to discuss a new and possibly brilliant idea.

#4: Challenge Norms

It's tough to question the status quo, policy, or what is "normal" at work. A creative influencer will always do that.

Why is this the way it is? Can we improve it? How can it be better? Those are the people you want on your creative team. They'll spot issues and solve them fast.

#5: Instincts

Creative influencers have good instincts about collaboration, who they want to work with, and why. Because they are quite playful people, if they don't like someone, you're going to know about it. These strong instincts help them make good decisions and then see them through to the end.

#6: Confidence

They aren't going to get anyone to believe in their idea if they don't believe in it first. These people may not be confident on the outside, but they are confident about work and what they can do in your team. Listen to them.

#7: Systemic

Innovators are creative, and they establish systems to their process. They may have a hard time adapting to new rules, but they will, once given the reasoning. They like structure and, to that matter, like rules once it is part of the success formula.

#7: Calm

Regardless of the conditions, innovators have a sense of calmness under fire. Over time, you will identify those individuals who can handle multiple, high level lasts and conditions. These will be your go-to people once you have a running track record with your staff.

Team Dynamics and Talents

Unlocking the potential that lies deep inside each one of your team members will be one of the most difficult and rewarding experiences of your career. But you have to understand what influences the influencers if you're going to have a chance at getting them on your side.

Being or becoming innovative on the spot can create a lot of pressure. That pressure can mount depending on the implications felt by an individual, team, or organization as a whole. The risks and desires by all stakeholders will set the tone for internal and external pressure, this will influence output performance. The best way to strengthen team dynamics lies in your ability to identify the best practices in creating an effective culture. These influences are based on intrinsic and extrinsic conditions.

Intrinsic Conditions *(These are the ones that influence internal desires):*

- **Motivation** – Bertrand Russell, the world-class mathematician and logician, determined that human beings are motivated by goals, not by the pleasure people experience when they attain those goals. This is important to understand because pleasure is infinitely desired, but goals are not. Once you understand that goals are the pathways to fulfillment, this can be the motivation to electrify your teams.
- **Competence** – Competence is very important to creative people and their ability to express their skill sets. Knowledge, skill, and performance are key enticements as is the gathering of new information, developing new skills, and exceeding perceived performance expectations. Give employees the vision for acquiring these elements; you may find the perfect formula for reward, intrinsically!
- **Autonomy** – Self-determination stems from the internal drive that motivates a person's will to perform and achieve. Autonomy and competence are joined together

as this trait too is a motivational element that innovators need to feel. It is the need to drive oneself to achieve for the team or organization.

- **Relatedness** – This is the universal want to interact, be connected to, and experience caring for others. We want to work in teams, tribes, and communities. Being a part of a winning team is even better. Remember our earlier example of those connected to Google and their intrinsic reward of being a part of that brand?

Extrinsic Conditions *(These are external factors affecting your team):*

Extrinsic motivation refers to motivation that comes from outside an individual. These motivating factors are external or outside, rewards, such as money, bonuses, or titles. These rewards provide satisfaction and pleasure that the task itself may not provide.

An extrinsically motivated person will work on a task even when they have little interest in it because of the anticipated satisfaction they will get from some reward. The rewards can be something as significant as "employee of the month" or big bucks.

Extrinsic motivation does not mean, however, that a person will not get any pleasure from working on or completing a task. It just means that the pleasure they anticipate from some external reward will continue to be a motivator even when the task to be done holds little or no interest. An extrinsically motivated employee, for example, may dislike a task, but the possibility of a good bonus will be enough to keep the individual motivated in order for him or her to put forth the effort to do well on a task.

- **Financial Rewards** – Commissions, bonuses, stock options, and employee stock plans are compensatory rewards used to motivate employees. Within the range of extrinsic motivations, these are "carrots." The drive for money and success can often motivate individuals but is not always sustaining for the innovator.
- **Praise and Recognition** – Studies have shown that recognition and praise go a long way in developing satisfaction. Delivering sincere and genuine compliments is a strong extrinsic motivational method.
- **Peer Pressure** – In the work environment, peer pressure to learn, keep up with peers and work harder, stay later, or take shorter lunches is a key contributor to motivation. This can be used to your benefit when you identify the key influencer. I tend to drop seeds of praise of others' performances in order to raise the bar of individuals that need it or that I think I can get more out of.
- **Consequences** – When the heat's on, many people take action or step up their performance. Knowing the boss will be angry or their job may be on the line is a reason many people get their work done. Is fear the best motivational tool in the arsenal? Use carefully because the effects can be an anti-motivator.

The Innovative Physical Environment

The environment that you work in can also have an effect on performance, thus there are several factors that enhance creativity in a work environment: climate, culture, leadership style, resources and skills, and structure and systems.

The creative and innovative behaviors at work seem to be promoted by a combination of both personal qualities and work environment factors. Work environment factors that promote creativity are: a feeling of shared, clearly-specified objectives, as well as a possibility to challenge; exchange of opinions or ideas; constructive controversies; freedom; challenges at work; trust and safety; team participation and collaborative idea flow; and open relationships between colleagues, as well as between supervisor and subordinates.

Creativity and innovation depend on the free flow of information. Creative work requires enormous concentration, and people require flexibility so they can have some personal downtime when needed to reboot.

Immediate environment or physical décor may seem like something that doesn't matter—but it does if you're looking for a creative response out of your employees. Beautiful creative surroundings are inspiring and, in turn, inspire— which improves creativity in work projects.

If you can change some simple things such as furniture, wall colors, and special features and create special social "chill" rooms where people can go for a break to chat and relax, then you'll find that the creative influencers become more active.

Even the space around a desk can improve or decrease creativity. Cubicles are the least creatively stimulating, unless you can customize them with images of your own. Aside from the décor and general surroundings, the people definitely matter the most. If you want teams to learn to work well together, then put them in similar areas at work.

Encourage them to become friends or to take breaks at the same time. This will allow them to form personal relationships outside of work, which could help them connect and become better at sharing work-based ideas and concepts.

When it comes to team dynamics and talents in creativity, you really want to put people in a position of power where their specific talent will shine. An employee that is known for coming up with great ideas while they take notes at a meeting should be encouraged to do this. An employee that flows well with one other person should spar ideas with them.

There will always be politics in team or office environments. The key is to get that out as much as possible. Creativity really is about fun, relaxing, and allowing an idea to take root in your mind and develop. This is what you want your team to learn.

Harnessing the Power of Diversity

Cultural diversity is often claimed to be a source of richness and a catalyst of processes of creativity and innovation. This is a relationship between diversity and creativity. In the tech sector, there are numerous intercultural, heterogeneous teams that naturally occur. The perspective value seems to be enormous and potentially undervalued at times. The power of the team could be that trigger for creativity that helps transform diversity into a source of innovation.

Different views, perspectives, outlooks, and ideas are best formulated from a diverse team. The saying goes, "Diversity is the mother of creativity," and people say that for a reason. They understand that when completely different minds begin to flow together, magic happens.

In groups, creativity, especially diversity, is a must-have. If you're going to create a new product or technology, then to get those rare and wonderful breakthroughs, you'll need diverse viewpoints. But how do you, as the manager, leader, or CEO, harness the power of diversity to result in a fully creative team of exceptional individuals?

1. We all perceive things differently, and because we need our perceptions to process data, a problem is better solved when more than one type of mind does it.
2. We are all creative in our own ways, which forces us to use outside perceptions and experiences and encourage

our minds to look outside of the box for the not-so-easy information that only exists if you know where to find it.

3. Your team will become more aware of the views and perceptions of others, which is quite an inspiring step within the context of their own thoughts, resulting in even more creative solutions to tough problems.

4. Learning is constant. Members will learn from each other and replicate skills and styles that best serve the behavior of the group.

5. There is power in cultural diversity in that it too provides a perspective that all can learn from and grow. This can have the most influence on the innovative and creative perspective if recognized and cultivated purposely.

6. Diversity doesn't only mean race; it can mean age, gender, sexual orientation, gender identity, body art or any differentiating characteristics. These are irrelevant in today's professional environment, or any number of other stereotypes that are protected under law. A blonde–haired, blue-eyed woman may seem to be a stereotype, but actually be extremely bright and creative.

If you want to harness the power of diversity, you have to build your teams with diverse people in them, keeping these details in mind:

- They must all get along.
- There must be no major personality clashes.
- Avoid loudmouths that will dominate all meetings.
- The willingness to share, connect, and create is essential.
- Respect among all team members regardless of diversity is the basis for working together.

You can help by telling your new teams that if there are any issues to please let you know about them. Especially in the tech field, where people work so closely together and are so involved in each other's projects, this is essential.

So you're looking for different thoughts, learning styles, values, attitudes, ideas, resources, and access to information. Create a creative group like this and there will be no project you can't conquer. You were born to create!

The Flawed Corporate Environment

Creativity has always been somewhat important to corporations, but creative people tend to be branded and separated from the herd. Instead of bringing them together, they are torn apart—quite literally by little white cubicles.

Processes that contain creative tasks are very different from the flawed business environment we are sometimes forced to function in today. Risk, team collaboration, and flexibility are three traits that define a creative orientated business.

The goal, of course, is to make sure that these creative processes get integrated into the business processes of old, influencing and changing them for the better. Right now, the flawed corporate environment wants a few things from you, their employee:

1. Sit down, do your work, do what we tell you, take orders.
2. Follow the strict business policy or process system.
3. Be as productive as you can so that they can make more money.
4. Nothing matters but meeting your quota and scraping by.

It's shocking that a person can work for 10 years at the same company and never get acknowledged or promoted. But it happens every day. The businesses out there are flawed. They don't understand that we are individuals who perform better when we are allowed to express ourselves.

Did you know that one of the Google offices has a slide in it from the top to the bottom floor? Google says it helps their employees release stress and have a bit of fun at the same time. Fun, excitement, happiness—these are all essential creative emotions that have been crushed out of the average employee's job.

You need to understand that if you are going to seize creative control of your company, then a lot is going to have to change. As you're reading this, I bet you're thinking of the several ways you treat your employees wrongly. Don't get me wrong—employees need work, deadlines, structure, and a time schedule.

What they don't need is undue pressure, authority that kills creativity, no involvement in the business outside of their jobs, and little to no reward for being people—not just drones. And that's essentially it. When you treat people like drones, they behave like drones. They walk in, day after day, mindlessly doing their jobs without even thinking.

All of that incredible creative juice, that power—wasted! Even a small team of five people can accomplish some amazing things by putting their minds together and being creative. While there are many micro activities your employees will have to perform on a daily basis, give them a reason to love their jobs.

If they can get to work, look forward to your creative meeting, be brimming with ideas and more—loving their acceptance and how people listen to their opinions—job satisfaction, happiness, and fulfillment are close behind. That means productivity and more money—the way that you're supposed to get it.

Reject your cold, clinical, unsocial, uncreative business of the past. It's a dying breed. Instead, embrace creativity and the people that so willingly offer it to you for your personal and business benefit.

Living Outside the Corporate Norms

For some, the corporate environment is not the best creative structure. Looking for efficiencies, flexibility, and individual accountability may come in a different form. This worked for one individual I have known for many years whose main purpose was to remove the walls of corporate constraints. And for him, this was the only way to achieve his ultimate goals.

Early on, John Brier, CEO of Tinbu, learned that backing out the numbers provided a deliberate and meaningful understanding for money. Equally important, he observed that everyone would spend given the right conditions. This has become the cornerstone for this high performance entrepreneur.

There were valuable lessons learned when John was in high school in Arlington, Massachusetts. Once, at the age of 15, he was asked by happenstance to work as a local carnival game tender, managing the ring toss area, the one with Coke bottles and small bagel rings, for 20% of what he earned. He says that this early experience gave him the "taste" to make money and the understanding that everyone has a "turning-point" for making a decision to spend his or her money, regardless of their personal background or financial circumstances. "*I was making sometimes $300 a day, a lot of money then. I saw that everyone comes to a carnival with the need to spend their money as they have already mentally budgeted an amount they will spend on games and rides and food when they arrive. It was my job to convince them that my game had the most value.*"

He would count the number of people passing his booth, think about each as having at least $20 to spend and that if he could get them to try one game with him for $2, he could get them to spend $6 ultimately. This was usually with a baker-dozen of more rings and a few throw techniques to help the customer.

"This was such a fun cash business that I once thought about buying part of the carnival as I got older," he recalls.

John continued to work with the family that owned the midway games through high school and college. That early introduction to making money and learning about consumer behavior became the catalyst for nearly 17 businesses since. The same principles then were easily applied to other businesses like mall retail traffic, wholesale distribution, and e-commerce.

Over the years, Brier has gone on to earn his M.B.A., and he served in the U.S. Army and National Guard. After 26 years post-college graduation, he owns four houses in a couple of different countries and manages several small enterprises in the U.S. and internationally. He jet-sets between each and likes the lifestyle of managing multiple projects simultaneously. When asked what his methods are for managing his diverse group of enterprises he states, *"Being entrepreneurial allows me the flexibility and freedom to innovate and experiment. I am always trying to protect my interests with other ventures. The digital world allows me to be available regardless of where I am. This is a very efficient way to keep control and scale my businesses when I see fit. I have about 95% more freedom to innovate than a Wall Street trader. I prefer this lifestyle!"*

John says, *"I enjoy the process of seeing what will happen. I like serving as the quarterback and allowing others the opportunity to do their job. The hard part is that not all employees have the same motivation as I do, and sometimes that is a disappointment. However, sometimes you get the right players together, and we can produce more wins than losses. That is the name of the game in my opinion."* He sums up his methods as, *"The more wisdom I gain, I am able to assemble the right processes and people early and get traction quickly to see if this is a good business or not. All in all, I know that you have to create and innovate to remain viable. When you stop reinvesting in new products and opportunities, you will eventually lose the revenue.*

If we are to keep thriving, we will continue to reinvest and innovate to meet my and our investors' expectations."

CHAPTER 4

Creative Control Structures

"It amazes me sometimes that even intelligent people will analyze a situation or make a judgment after only recognizing the standard or traditional structure of a piece."

DAVID BOWIE

In your business, you may wish you had that differentiating element that separates you from your competition or makes you an even better business leader. With the correct understanding for the creative control structures, you could experience and begin to expect revived growth from your pool of human assets. Very soon the success of your business will rely on the creative potential output of your employee base.

Defining the Creative Control Structures

A creative control structure is simply a structure or group of plans that you will have to implement to transform your business culture from low or moderately innovative to highly creative. Right now your business has many systems, and like any good company, you continue to challenge your business practices in order to optimize outcomes. Rules change, new generations of employees emerge, and technologies redefine the work environment, and your ability to adapt and lead is more crucial than it has ever been.

While some of your operational practices are tried and true, evolving practices to meet current conditions will help calibrate revenues, efficiencies, and differentiation to new levels. Marissa Mayer, the new CEO of Yahoo, who was an executive at Google prior to this, has reported that she has taken drastic new steps in managing the company. Due to the financial expectations of managing a public company and competitive pressures, as CEO, she is controlling every aspect of the hiring process at Yahoo and has put an end to virtual offices, calling everyone back to work or quit. To that regard, she reviews every top-level executive to assure they meet her criteria (e.g., longer hours, product delivery, and new product development processes). Also, she found that virtual employees, those working from home, were not logging into the company VPN, thus serving as the catalyst for the end of off-site working. While this may seem a bit unorthodox for the technology sector today, with the access to virtual tools, the need for systemic control and performance change is critical. These steps could have both positive and potentially negative repercussions on the company.

These changes have not been received well by the press and have created a fragile work environment. As a result, Yahoo's ability to attract highly effective senior managers to the company and new progressive innovators may become limited.

Conversely, it may be the bold moves that make the difference in this highly competitive environment. While that is yet to be seen, the bold moves are a practice highly valued during these economic times.

The future potential of your business does rest in the hands of your current management team and employees. What is their creative aptitude as compared to your competitors? Could you use a re-design of output and expectations? Does your business measure innovation effectiveness and creative output? What are the financial implications to not making change? How does reward encourage creative output?

If you haven't begun to think of these game-changing issues, now is the time. To seize creative control and start a new movement in your company that brings prosperity and income to everyone means that you need to create some creative control structures.

Creative Control Structure 1 – The Strategic Mirror

The challenge faced by most companies is defining and anchoring their strategic vision at every level of the company. Every aspect of new innovation should mirror that vision. With that clearly established and defined, every individual within the company knows that every initiative, strategy, and tactic should mirror the strategic vision. You and your staff should know how to "elevator pitch" that vision in not more than three sentences. With that clarity, any new creative and innovative vision should support that strategic objective.

Creative Control Structure 2 – The Leadership Factor

With the foundation established around strategic vision, leaders will need to connect to the ultimate outcome of that vision. Leadership from the top down or bottom up is necessary so that all have ownership in each creative initiative. If your company was the inventor of the iPhone, what leadership principles led everyone to that final outcome? It was necessary for all to reflect the strategic mirror within their leadership support structure.

Creative Control Structure 3 – Exploration

This step in the process for achieving creative control is the most intriguing for most people. It is where you begin to investigate processes, solutions, functions, and alternatives. Exploration as a structure is the process by which we discover the individual, the teams, the groups, and their ability to explore the many aspects of solutions, process, and differentiation.

Creative Control Structure 4 – Synthesize

When you *synthesize*, you combine two or more things to create something more complex, more compelling; an adaptation of old and new, outdated and updated, passé and chic. There is a never-ending supply of innovation that can be synthesized out of existing products and the call for extreme product revolution. There are sunk cost advantages and product evolution efficiencies as a subset of advantages.

Creative Control Structure 5 – Ownership

Here is where we attach everyone in our company to the development process. All will have some ownership in our strategy, product line, advocation, and final results (success or failure). From early in our discussion in this book, ownership has been mentioned as the glue that adheres the individual to the group, the group to the team, and, ultimately, teams to the company. We all strive to attach ourselves to success and winners. We will be that agent that involves us to the end result, particularly the successful innovations. Here we shape the environment, the internal and external impression, and everyone wants to be connected to it.

Integrating these principles into your staff and teams will become an art, and you'll be able to experience what it's like to leverage different people's creativity and talents across the organization, large or small.

Assessing Talent for Perfect Innovation

Ultimately, we are only as good as the people around us. We cannot be great because of one person; we must all be great. In this harsh competitive environment, it's not enough to be just "good" at your job anymore. Your competitors take this very seriously, and they are making darn sure that they hire the best and fire people that don't fit into the new creative dynamic. This is how you need to start perceiving your human assets.

Either they contribute something special to the mix or they need to move on. It sounds harsh, but in business, competition is harsh, and you can't afford to play the game with a losing team. In fact, even something as small as a bad attitude can corrupt an entire team.

The hiring and, for that matter, the firing process needs to fit in with your new "creative-first" ideology. You cannot afford to sacrifice creativity for good staff members anymore. They have to be both—creative and team-orientated with a positive attitude! Obviously, it helps if your business has a reputation as being a creative company. You will naturally attract innovative types that thrive in creative environments.

And that's what you want! You'll find that your interviews are more diverse, interesting, and in-depth than when you were looking for straightforward, educated employees. Put experience, age, and education behind you—because creativity has just become your number one hiring criteria. Work on your business culture, mission, and the type of work you do to get the best people.

Innovators that apply will do so because they've heard you're working on cutting edge stuff or have done something truly creative in the field that they want to do. It's these people who you want to impress enough to come and work for you.

Firing, on the other hand, takes some guts. Sometimes you'll change your business culture and realize just how little some people do—even though they've been with your company for several years. It's up to you whether to fire them or not, but I'll say this, there is no point keeping uninspiring, boring people that don't create for your company.

Talent Acquisition

It's true that the future of your company rests in the hands of a chosen few, but don't worry—the good news is you get to handpick them! I'm not talking about hiring new people; I'm talking about recognizing rare creative talent that you've already hired and potentially missed. Trust me; right now there are many excellent high performers in your company who are hidden away and ready to give you their full capacity.

When you're looking to find creative talent, you have to keep a few things in mind. First of all, the innovative, high capacity workers could be hiding away—content to work for their salary. Sometimes they won't be top performers at first or people who make any sort of impact on your business. They just need to be given the opportunity to shine. You need to create opportunities in the workplace that will unmask these special people.

If a creative and innovative person is under a lot of stress or has a controlling boss, he or she may be working at a low capacity. Their high capacity output is suppressed. These people tend to hold back when they feel unappreciated or stifled. These hidden jewels are something empathetic, which is a valuable trait for establishing creative team dynamics. They are often able to place themselves in the shoes of other people, which make them a force to be reckoned with when trying to come up with things that sell. They ask for help because they aren't afraid to learn, and they always have questions that need to be answered.

You have to open your mind and consider the possibility that creativity comes from all sorts of strange places. Whatever their position, you need to uncover and harness their talent to improve your innovative output. We are looking for those with high potential for performance.

Methods for identifying underachieving talent are:

1. Stimulate the innovation quotient.
2. Step up performance criteria.
3. Take control of talent development.
4. Push top performers to new challenges.
5. Change recognition and reward.
6. Involve young leaders early.
7. Evaluate and challenge.

- **Stimulating the innovation quotient** is the process of making sure the achievers and underutilized are constantly excited about the future. They need to be involved and challenged. You have to concern yourself with the elite performers as much as you need to cultivate the under-utilized. Their desire to achieve is not dissimilar. They need to be intellectually challenged.
- **Performance criteria** are the measurements for "raising the bar" of output. Quality is far more important than quantity, but the expectation lies in the elite and under recognized individuals to emulate, learn, challenge, and

be thought of as high performers. Unless you continue to set new achievement levels, they will get bored or entrench to a cruising altitude.

- **Taking control of the talent development** should not be left to direct supervisors. It needs to be part of the asset maintenance and development program. Senior management needs to make this a high priority so that team building, retention, and support are as important as a direct line to revenue.

- **Pushing top performers** to new challenges is the best way to keep these elite assets interested in their work; at the same time it sets the pace for the entire company. Just as important is the recognition of achievement.

- **Change recognition and reward** is an important step in not letting the reward and recognition factor lose its importance. While plaques, money, and ceremony are all important to the recognition of top performers, the what, where, who, and when should be changed up to keep it interesting and exciting for those that follow and wish to look for that achievement.

- **Involve young leaders** early so they get a taste of higher level planning in the C-Suite. This effort keeps you close to new achievers and helps you to monitor your new asset growth. Engage them from time to time in management projects as this will serve as reward, acknowledgement, and goals for others to achieve high levels of output and performance.

- **Evaluate and challenge** is perceived as the annual dusting work or a "must do" HR effort to give salary or bonuses, but really should be used as an asset maintenance effort. It is so important to making sure you are retaining and setting new benchmarks with the elite core, and you need to use this as a critical effort that is reported to investors and the board.

Building your team is not about finding just the elite group of people—it's about finding people who are willing to share, work together, and collaborate for the good of the business. They will be willing to open up and create—and you should be willing to do the same. Whether you know it or not, you are drawn to creativity.

When talent presents itself in your current employee ranks, identify it, challenge it, and integrate it. You may be resting on a goldmine of creative talent that has a potential to change your company dynamics. Keep a close eye at home first before searching outside to find new talent.

Team Behavior

As important as establishing the strategic vision is setting the criteria for proper behavior of team members. I have found this to be an vital tool for setting the stage for interaction and engagement. When introduced, I confer with all members, to confirm their acceptance and engage discussion around whether any of these principles are in conflict with their perspective.

1. We will always treat each other with respect.
2. We will develop personal relationships to enhance trust and open communication.
3. We value constructive feedback.
4. We will avoid being defensive and will give feedback in a constructive manner.
5. We will treat all members in the same way as valuable contributors.
6. We will recognize and celebrate individual and team accomplishments.
7. As team members, we will pitch in to help where necessary to help solve problems and catch up on behind schedule work.

8. We will never argue in public but will meet in private to discuss our concerns and will not leave until we have a resolution.

The most difficult thing to do in any new creative-orientated company is to select team members who are not only highly creative, but also work well together. Ideally, you'd like people who inspire each other, feed off each other, and produce excellent quality work. I've learned over the years that not all teams can do this.

Sometimes your team will be verbally sound, but they won't be able to produce the physical results that you need. In app development, for example, good ideas can often be too complex for the team to manage. In the idea stage, the concept is sound, even exciting—but when the team tries to mock up a demo, it becomes disastrous.

While this happens to the best of teams sometimes, you'll know if it becomes a trend in a team. You have to find the balance between thinkers and doers. A good creative is someone that comes up with an idea and is then able to bring this idea into the physical world. Without that final step, your team will fall apart.

You can damage team dynamics by introducing clashing personalities into the same team. Everyone needs to be affable and able to work together well in order for your creative team to work. Any sort of stress, bad feelings, or discomfort will reduce the creativity in your team. That means fewer great ideas and worse productivity.

Mixing and matching teams has really become an art for me. If there is a budget concern, for example, I might put the finance and design teams together to come up with a new product line that we can launch within the parameters of the business. When you do this, you're not only guaranteeing that your new product works well, but that it's financially viable too.

The most creative finance people working with your best creative design team are bound to come up with something incredible. You can even run their ideas past your other teams—like sales and marketing. Get the ball rolling on all sides by introducing all of your teams to one specific concept and wait for a few days.

Many people will come back and have something to contribute to the project. With that kind of fierce creative input, just imagine how much more successful your product launch will be —and it's all thanks to your teams. Mix them and match them, but make sure they work!

Testing the Process

There are several ways you can test whether you are heading in the right direction with your individual and team choices. These may seem like tests but more to the point of assessments.

The first is looking at the staff aptitude. This is a judgment for assessing ones aptitude for performance and potential:

1. Does the individual come to you with issues that they are ready to champion and take control of?
2. How often did they take the initiative to better the company?
3. What is the track record for accomplishments (wins versus losses)?
4. How are they at dealing with adversity?
5. Do peers perceive them as leaders?
6. What level of control are you willing to risk with this individual?

Once you have applied this list of questions to yourself and senior, middle, or new leaders, you will know where you see their potential in the company. If you are unable to answer any of the questions above, give it more time and put those individuals in situations where your answers become clear.

Identifying individuals early allows you to make the right hiring, firing, or promotion decisions. Be patient and do not lose the asset potential to early judgment.

It's not a race, however—success means different things to everyone. For the business, it may mean the commercial success of a particular app that was downloaded a million times. For the individual, it may be the best character design they've ever created. Whatever it is, don't forget to see creative people as individuals as well; after all, it's how they and your business ultimately thrive.

Optimize the Output

It's important that you take the lead in new ways to optimize the output of your innovation and product development teams. This means watching them and guiding them, but still allowing them to take point on creative projects. The last thing you want to do is stifle their creativity with too many rules.

Getting Systemic but Simple

When it comes to product development and new innovation, it is essential to focus on a structured and systematic approach to product design stages. The need for new product development and innovation is a must in this competitive consumer world in every aspect. The success of new products depends mostly on the new product development process. The teams assigned will be the differentiating influence on meeting goals and objectives.

Well-defined process system allows time for more creative interjection. Simplistic always wins when dealing with large or even small teams. Such processes involve:

1. Well-defined process inputs in the form of customer

needs and product specifications.

2. Well-defined process steps, process outputs (deliverable documents), and responsibilities.
3. The flexibility to support multiple processes and tailor the process to the particular project requirements.
4. Process templates to improve efficiency and improve consistency.
5. Process controls in the form of ownership reviews and design reviews.
6. A defined set of stages to meet deliverables.
7. Task breakdown and deliverable documents associated with each stage.
8. A set of templates for the deliverable documents to support the process.

Getting Personal

Find out what makes your team tick. Speak to every single person individually and often. Get to know who they are as people—their strengths and weaknesses. Then you'll be able to make suggestions as the project moves forward.

Knowing your team well is the fastest route to creating a good creative company. Clear expectations and well defined job descriptions that articulate the creative and collaborative environment will set the first right impression. Combined with a good understanding for your employees from top-down and bottom-up will improve conditions and productive output from the get-go.

This is especially true of bosses and their employees. But to be a good creative manager, you have to be on top of who people are. It's individuals that will drive your business success, so this is imperative. What if promoting an especially gifted creative talent would cause him to come up with an idea so great it earns your company millions? Think about it!

That's why, to optimize your output, you need to be a creative-people person. Don't forget about your own creativity and your ultimate objective. You should be a part of the team, the leader, but you should behave as a team member. Creativity works best when it's offered freely, not coaxed. That's why strong leadership, scare tactics, and stress decrease creative ability.

The truly gifted creative types will always be in demand. Don't forget that you have to keep them happy, interested, and stimulated, because they can go anywhere and get a job. Businesses will often try to poach highly creative people from you, so be aware of that. To optimize your output, it's your job to make sure that your core creative team is happy.

When they are happy, they'll produce. If they don't work well together, are dissatisfied, or feel that they are mistreated in any way—they will leave. And here's the truth...if someone has been at your company for quite a while and has made friends, leaving encourages other people to leave for greener pastures.

Optimize your development team's output by being there for them, knowing who they are, and supporting them where and when you can. Don't be the traditional boss who strong-arms work out of your employees; it just won't work well for a creative team. Teach them to be fluid, inspired, and daring— and your creative team will reach for the stars!

CHAPTER 5

Why Contribution Trumps Ownership

"Creativity is just connecting things. When you ask creative people how they did something, they feel a little guilty because they didn't really do it, they just saw something. It seemed obvious to them after a while. That's because they were able to connect experiences they've had and synthesize new things."

STEVE JOBS

Early in my career, I worked as an analyst for a large insurance company. I eagerly put myself in positions to get strategic assignments in order to get noticed by senior management. I soon realized that I did it all wrong, focusing on myself as the one to get things done when in fact I should have focused on building the talent of my team and figuring out ways to enhance and express their productivity and output. This truly is the secret—make the team strong and you get noticed and are given bigger projects and more responsibility.

A product and development team nearly always owns what they do, and they are accountable for the ideas and the work they propose and provide, respectively. To that regard, individuals and the teams they support are ambassadors of their work. Those connected even in the smallest way are also contributors, in way of discussion, planning, and organizing.

Ownership vs. Contribution

There is a dividing line in business right now, especially in the tech field, that allows people to contribute, but also prevents them from taking the fall if something goes wrong. People tend to evade ownership of their ideas to prevent them from getting into trouble or from becoming a real part of the creative process.

Too often there are people that are happy to contribute and shirk ownership. This is not the best way and holds little ownership to the good, bad, and ugly. A good idea or good suggestions should be followed by a willingness to own their creative suggestions, to stand by them so that great work gets accomplished.

For the most part, technology professionals want to contribute. There is a reason they have selected a career where innovation, fast-changing conditions, huge competition, and high output is expected from all. There are no real hiders in the tech innovation field. They are the best and the brightest. They wish to be with others that inspire; those they can learn from and collaborate with successfully. They thrive for the potential to build something bigger than themselves. I have never seen so much worker pride since the digital revolution. That in itself inspires.

Perhaps your working environment still abides by the law of contribution instead of ownership. I expect every team member to contribute, and when they do, they must own their ideas and inspire the rest of the team with their vision. This is non-negotiable.

WHEN I CHANGED MY APPROACH, THE DYNAMIC CHANGED...

Focusing on creativity and contribution as a rule in meetings allows you to see how your team functions. You can spot those who generally produce very little but have lots to say; then those who are generally quiet but take on most of the real follow up work; and then those who only speak when they have the answer, usually great ideas.

To turn your team into a creative, innovation machine, you need to reverse the balance of the talkers, the non-doers, and the people who don't really want to contribute or own the ideas due to fear or accountability. All true innovators will stand behind their ideas because they have a real vision and ownership in what they produce. They want to protect, nurture, and drive for perfection. You want an army of this type!

Regardless, there are better ways to get higher performance. These techniques will encourage and open the high performer without your team even knowing what has occurred. They will just know there has been a difference and they feel good about it.

The Meeting

I learned how to work with product development teams early in my career when I was the data control director for a large hospital that was pushing tons of financial data across huge non-interoperable systems to financial institutions and international insurance companies. The development teams were compiled of the best of the best in the technology and data storage fields. The interesting thing was trying to get them to break down the walls of hierarchy in meetings. Most had learned the old-school approach of watching and waiting for the senior executive to give the game plan. It was very rare to get open contribution from all meeting members and almost never from junior attendees. It, however, only took me four meetings to reestablish and recalibrate the "meeting" to a "think team." Here is how I did it and have been doing it since.

The Think Team

1. Attach leader accountability.
2. Give three solution paths.
3. Identify two reasons why each path will work.
4. Identify two reasons why each path will not work.
5. Solve failure paths.
6. Gain consensus on one most efficient path.
7. Gain consensus on one most thorough solution path.
8. Build budget for both solutions (#6 and #7).
9. Present choices to management team.
10. Enter selected solution into the project pipeline.

#1: Attach Leader Accountability

This is an opportunity to switch up meeting leaders. You want to select a leader that will be closest to the problem and that has the most to gain from the solution. This is not the time to keep selecting management but a time to bring new owners to the table. Junior or not, this is the opportunity to draw out new performers. This role is responsible for setting the stage in advance with the attendees.

- Define the problem
- Provide the situation
- List expectations

Everyone is expected to participate in all 10 phases.

#2: Give Three Solution Paths

Solicit the group for solutions; the ones that seems most obvious. While time is money, do not rush to a conclusion. Prevent the participants that KNOW the answer and the ONLY way. That is old school, and we need to find the best solution within a reasonable investigation.

#3: Identify Two Reasons Why Each Path Will Work

The leader will develop discussion for reasoning why the three paths will work. The team will provide two qualifiable or quantifiable reasons for each path. This will force participations and output with sound reasoning.

#4: Identify Two Reasons Why Each Path Will Not Work

The leader will develop discussion for reasoning why the three paths will fail. The team will provide two qualifiable or quantifiable reasons for each path. This will force participations and output with sound reasoning for the failure. These can be used for contingency planning later in the development cycle.

#5: Solve Failure Paths

Being forced to solve the failure paths provides clear attempts to rule out or rethink the paths. These too serve as contingency solutions.

#6: Gain Consensus on One Most Efficient Path

The team is now asked to select what seems like the low-cost solution and teasing the efficiency attributes. This starts the budgetary and ROI phase.

#7: Gain Consensus on One Most Thorough Solution Path

The team is now asked to select what seems like the best-case solution without cost consideration. This starts the budgetary and ROI phase as well.

#8: Build Budget for Both Solutions (#6 and #7)

This is the phase for building the case from the discussion. It should all fall into place with the prior discussion. Email string for group signoff. No follow-up meeting required.

#9: Present Choices to Management Team

Getting senior management or review panel ownership with the meeting detail gets the solution to the pipeline quickly.

#10: Pipeline Solution

Based on ownership at all levels, everyone understands the problems, the 360 degree view of solutions, and has bought into the activity.

The Think Team is not just one team in the organization; it is a frame of mind. This process, used concisely, will build efficiency, thoroughness, and wide ownership with endurance.

Pushing Ownership

Pushing your team at the senior or mid-levels comes from different perspectives, with the results centered on ownership and contribution.

Whether you have grown your enterprise from a few full-time employees to a couple hundred, you are going to learn a few things along the way. You will probably ask yourself at some point, *"When and how can I let go of the things that I have been doing myself or directing others to do?"* Furthermore, you may ask, *"How do I get others in my organization to use their own business acumen to improve their business ownership without my daily involvement?"* This is a common dilemma among founders of both for-profit and nonprofit companies.

There is one company I have watched grow over the last 15 years and have admired its willingness to try new things in and outside of their core competencies. Volunteers of America Northern New England (VOANNE) is a company that encompasses a progressive energy, despite its conservative existence. Founded regionally in 1992 as an expansion effort by its national parent, Volunteers of America (founded in 1896), its CEO and regional founder, June Koegel, knows how to get things done with very little resources.

Today VOANNE is the model of innovation for the entire corporate Volunteers of America organization. June bases this outward perception on the decentralized nature of the organization. *"This allows us to not be caught up in process and procedures. It allows us more agility in course correction when needed. This is probably not the most formative environment to work under, but it has allowed us the flexibility as a smaller enterprise to find and take on new opportunities,"* she states.

June says about hiring, *"I have been known to tell people that if they do not like change, then this is not the right place for them."* The company is partially funded by a combination of grants, government programs, and donations. *"If we are not looking 360 degrees at any given moment, another social service organization will take the funding. That means we have to be better than our competitors in follow-through. This wins new business for us and keeps existing programs working."*

When asked how she inspires the innovation that other peer Volunteers of America branches admire, she states, *"It lies in my practice to not go too deep into the weeds with my senior team. Once I am pulled into the deep details of a situation, I find that I start making decisions that my senior team should be making, they start relying on me to make all decisions, and then the innovation and change starts to slow down. For the sake of their personal accountability and my bandwidth, I need to stay at the 30,000-foot perspective. This keeps everyone on their game."*

A recent Harvard study on creativity and problem-solving in the workplace suggests that people are at their most creative when they are happy and progressing well in their projects.

Progression and a general feeling of wellbeing are two of the strongest motivating forces they discovered after analyzing thousands of pieces of data.

Your meetings should therefore serve as a time when people in your planning, product, development, or innovation team can propose solutions to current problems during a project— while you positively reinforce how far they've come with the work. Your job as a manager is to put them at ease and stimulate a non-judgmental environment where ownership can be taken easily.

Encouraging contribution in meetings is key to the core concept of building an innovative environment for your business. According to an article on MSNBC, meetings are not a productive environment for creativity, but they should be! Just because every team member is different and will respond to different environments doesn't mean your meetings are doomed forever.

I call this the "creative stimulation effect" —by giving the team the problem scope in advance and then allowing them some time to think about it on their own before the meeting. The objective is to make it clear that everyone should have an opinion in the process. John Cleese chalks this method up to allowing the intelligent subconscious to work on the problem in its own time.

A creative mind will use conscious thought to come up with solutions. Then, as the day goes by, the subconscious mind will add to that solution, improving it. When a meeting is called to order, everyone has had a chance to truly mull over the issues, or the new product, or whatever. What results is a lot more creative than simply calling a meeting.

This is the most important set up method that I use to get more accountability from my team. Because each individual has to pitch his or her idea or solution to the team, they are forced to take ownership of their own ideas. It works out better for the company, as we are able to use our creative workforce better.

The Attendee Perspective

Understand the invitee perspective in order to effectively manage a meeting. To that regard, it is also the responsibility of the attendee to understand why, who, what, and where and be fully loaded in advance. These are the issues that each should be fully engaged to understand:

1. Understand your role and why you are invited.
2. You know who the other attendees are and why they are invited.
3. You should read the Think Team papers and prepare in advance...fully!
4. Gain clarity in advance so you are completely prepared.
5. Arrive on time, without your mobile phone or other distractions.
6. Participate as both an excellent listener and contributor.
7. Follow the meeting rules and serve as an ambassador of the rules.
8. Follow up with any appointed work on time and professionally.
9. Keep abreast through the meeting and product cycle.

Verbal vs. Physical Contribution

There is one other issue that I'd like to bring to your attention that significantly affects how your team functions as a cohesive unit. In a study published in *Creativity and Innovation Management*, the authors discovered that confidence was in fact a key element in the creative process.

Your employees can't become more confident if they don't accept ownership of their ideas, suggestions, and work. That's where collaboration becomes tricky. Do meetings work as they are now? Yes. Is this how you should be running a creative team? No. People will collaborate as long as it's their job, even if they're bad at it.

What you need to do as their manager is unlock the verbal and physical contribution that lies in each one of your employees. Everyone has the potential to be creative given the work environment is consciously prepared for collaboration and contribution.

Confidence is extremely important in creating a creative environment—where your team members can flourish and expand their talents. Employees who have faith in their own creative abilities have proven that they use them more often. If you want more creativity in your teams, then you need to start rewarding individual members for their contributions.

A verbal contribution in a meeting environment is important because it can inspire the rest of your team members to see things in a different light. Everyone's brains work differently, and while one person may not be able to come up with a great idea alone, if coupled with another team member, they could be brimming with excellent ideas.

Creative people feed off each other in this way, so when you improve their verbal and physical contribution, the creative potential of your team will also improve. Keep in mind that different team members will struggle with these changes at first. For someone who does not like public speaking, verbal communication in a meeting could make them uncomfortable.

This discomfort will reduce their creative output, which will result in undeveloped ideas and an overall decline in productivity. Interestingly, the above study also found that highly creative people were also somewhat unstructured—

preferring to remain agile or flexible with their workday.

If you had to ask me which is more important, verbal or physical contributions, I'd have to say both are part of the process—one can't exist without the other. Creativity and contribution to the solution begins at the verbal stage and is developed and expressed in the physical. But if you leap over the best verbal ideas, you'll never get a good physical result.

Imagine a team of 10 people. Sounds great for solution generation, doesn't it? What if I told you the real stats on this team were three people contributing ideas, five people helping to develop those ideas, and two people doing most of the work for the settled upon idea. Suddenly, this team doesn't seem effective at all. Most teams are like this!

But if you can unleash the creative potential in each person and use all 10 people—for a 10-person verbal discussion, then use all 10 people to create the finished product—wow! You end up with an incredible end result. The trick is to get this kind of creative productivity out of your employees. It begins with those core elements—confidence, acknowledgement, encouragement—and allowing them enough time to think outside of meetings.

Individual vs. Company Goals

Why are some teams so dysfunctional you may ask? Easy—employees align themselves with personal goals and not the goals of the strategic vision. They see the company as their "work" and a way to make money, but some do not see the company as an extension of who they are or what they can achieve.

As we discussed in Chapter 4, the glue to wide ownership lies in the strategic vision. Ownership, or lack of it, is the fundamental reason why there may be a lack of contribution. *Forbes* reported that, according to a Multiple Generations @

Work survey[3] of 1,189 employees and 150 managers, 91% of Millennials (born between 1977 and 1997) expect to stay in a job for less than three years. That means they expect to have over 15 jobs in their lifetime! If the expectation is short stays and the company projects this belief, ownership is also limited.

With these kinds of stats stacked against you, how are you ever supposed to train your staff to align their goals with the goals of your company? With creative contribution, of course.

In for Life

Once a person's DNA is part of the innovation environment, they are in for life, so to speak. This means that your company can rapidly improve these numbers by validating the talents of your employees and getting them to contribute, own their involvement, and love being a part of the company culture.

Individual goals may be to earn more money, get promoted, learn new skills, or win company awards. Company goals, on the other hand, are completely different. Companies need to make more money, create better products, become more competitive, improve workplace productivity, and most of all, be better than their competitors.

Imagine if you could make these your employees' goals. Aligning individual and company goals is a task that most managers overlook. Work is seen as something you do, and you're paid for it. The end. But that's not what makes an incredible company tick. Employees at Google, for example, are very happy and creatively fulfilled. Right? If they are contributing, they are.

To make sure that your employees' creative abilities are

---

3   Meister, Jeanne. Job Hopping Is the 'New Normal' for Millennials: Three Ways to Prevent a Human Resource Nightmare. http://www.forbes.com/sites/jeannemeister/2012/08/14/job-hopping-is-the-new-normal-for-millennials-three-ways-to-prevent-a-human-resource-nightmare/

fully realized, their goals have to be aligned with the vision of your company. To do this, make it clear what your goals are for each project, and clue them in to the bigger picture.

Top-down/Bottom-up Techniques

Top-down planning is sometimes referred to as senior strategic planning. Top-down project planning is focused on keeping the decision making process at the senior level. Goals and milestones are established at the top level, and those at the top are not often willing to take advice or any guidance from lower level employees. Senior managers must provide clarity as much as possible when establishing expectations since those responsible for the plan were not involved in the planning process. Morale can fall short when the team is not involved in the planning process and progress can be driven by fear. If you recall my earlier example of David Norton dealing with the decline in customer spending at Harrah's (Caesars) due to the 2008 global financial crisis, he felt that urgent situation required a top-down technique.

With top-down planning, management chooses techniques to align projects and goals. Senior management holds the sole responsibility for the plans set forth and for the end result. This way of thinking assumes that management has the most ownership to plan and carry out a project. While this may limit contribution from talented employees that may have more experience with certain aspects of the project, it takes a more exclusive approach. This technique allows management to divide a project into steps and then into still smaller steps. And this continues until the steps are analyzed and then assigned to a project manager. Top-down approach is typically used on long-term goals. Short-term, emergency needs can sometimes lose priority. I have no problem with this approach when it is applied to small projects.

Bottom-up planning is referred to as a tactical initiative. Since more employees are involved within their area of expertise, a project gets deeper attention. Team members all have input during each stage of the process. Initiatives are developed at the core levels and are then passed up to the next higher level. Senior management is pitched and asked for approval. The example in this chapter of June Koegel from Volunteers of America Northern New England attributed this approach to more ownership and accountability from her management team.

Ownership from the bottom-up approach on the projects is more likely since lower-level employees are involved in planning. Staff is more motivated and morale is higher than the top-down approach since they have a stake in the planning. While project managers are ultimately responsible for the completion of the project, management still has the final responsibility for checks and balances.

Balancing Approaches: The best-case scenario of a combination of these two project management principles is most effective. The strength of each approach has a place, and you can align each so that the needs fit the case. You, management, can assess where best to fit ownership and approach. With a combination, you can merge the vision of management with the skills of lower-level employees. This allows the project to be completed more efficiently and lets a company exercise its employee strength.

Creating Harmonious Collaboration

Teams are naturally harmonious—and they can collaborate like champions. This is because creativity breeds creativity, and innovation breeds innovation. If you can change the environment and how your employees perceive themselves in your company, you can work towards this level of creative collaboration.

Think of your team as a unit. Everyone is supposed to have a role or a function. Some of these functions are the same—such as coming up with solutions. Some of these are unique—like a special ability that one team member has. It's your job to make sure that each team member is inspired and is using their creativity to assist you in your projects.

WHEN PEOPLE TAKE OWNERSHIP OF THEIR IDEAS...

That's when they are at their best. This "fight to be the best" culture is not the solution. Put everyone on equal ground and on equal footing. Move up on assignment and responsibility as it warrants. Assign work to teams and individuals with the vision of using the productivity as an asset. Always look to build the confidence of the players in your company for harmonious collaboration.

I had a new employee, Alex, who came into his own on a complex project we were working on for three months. Over those months, Alex engaged and contributed more and more, and his ideas became central to our project. Finally, I promoted him to team leader as I discovered his incredible ability to inspire creativity, trust, and inclusion in teams and among his peers. This was necessary as part of my plan to recognize, reward, and include excellence as part of our innovation environment plan.

Contribution trumps ownership when creativity meets collaboration. Up until this point, team members feel possessive about their ideas. They need to get to the stage when they know that their ideas belong to their team for the good of the business. When their goals align with the strategic vision and when their creativity is at their peak, they will become highly productive.

Your goal, as always, is to get the most creativity out of every single one of your employees. They must learn to contribute superb ideas and even better practical work to be a strong team member. There is no such thing as "coasting by" anymore. This makes them unaccountable and possessive of their creativity.

Begin by allowing your team to get to know each other on a personal level. You want to build your team out of people that work well together creatively. Everyone should be a leader in their own right. Yes, you'll have a team leader that takes point in the meeting—but everyone should understand that their ideas are all relevant and important. I love getting people together quarterly for paintball, race tracks, or any activity that lets people individualize a part of them not seen in the workplace.

Create harmonious collaboration by unleashing the creative potential in each of your team members. Get them to contribute more, and soon you'll see just how valuable a team of productive individuals can be if they all work equally on a project.

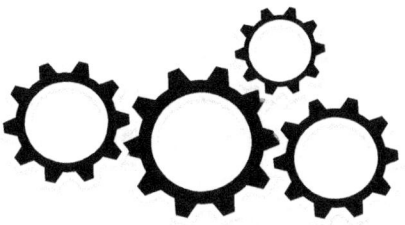

CHAPTER 6

The Dynamic System of Creation

"I do not think there is any thrill that can go through the human heart like that felt by the inventor as he sees some creation of the brain unfolding to success... such emotions make a man forget food, sleep, friends, love, everything."

NIKOLA TESLA

If you have not studied the biography of Nikola Tesla, take the time to do so. He was a Serbian-American inventor, electrical engineer, mechanical engineer, physicist, and futurist best known for his contributions to the design of the modern alternating current (AC) electrical supply system. He filed over 300 patents.

While Thomas Edison gets most of the public credit as the inventor of the electronic age, Nikola Tesla was the one who had most of the ideas that led to a significant impact. Tesla actually worked for Edison during his early years.

Unfortunately, Edison was better at patenting ideas, an area that Tesla lacked as an inventor during his early years.

Nikola Tesla had amazing visual thinking powers. When he got an idea for a new machine, he was able to "set it up" in his mind, visualize it starting, and leave it running to see how it would work. His ability was so developed and the results that he perceived in his mind were so accurate that when it came to building a prototype for a new machine, it reacted as it did in his mind. He would already know exactly how it would perform because of his "Mind Lab" experiments.

Your company is made up of bright, articulate people; you feel it when those people are performing at their peak performance. But what you want is to push them to even fuller experiences and gratification within their work environment. You want to give them the opportunity to create something new and the ability to contribute to the creation of something important. Perhaps you are sitting on a Nikola Tesla!

The very height of creativity is invention, but this innovation doesn't just happen overnight. You need to create a dynamic system of creation within your company and fix these core concepts to the heart of every team that creates for you.

Moving from Static to Dynamic Collaboration

To be static in a team means that many people are unmoving, silent, and noncontributory. As I mentioned before, people will always be forced to collaborate if it's their job. But being forced to do something and doing something with excitement and inspiration are two completely different things.

For example, team A is made up of five people. This is a static, "old school" team. There is the team leader who comes up with 80% of the ideas and strategies. There is the "go-to" guy who works on making these ideas a reality. Everyone else simply goes along with the plans, doing the bare minimum they can. They like to do as little as possible.

Team B is made up of five people as well. This is a dynamic, creative team. All of them are equal, and they are charged with coming up with ideas, suggestions, or solutions for a particular project. They share in meetings, inspire each other, and work together verbally and physically to make the project a reality. They are highly creative and give their all to each project.

Which team do you think is the most successful? Team B, is right! And there is a simple reason for that. You have to be happy and motivated to create, and you have to create to become happy and motivated. It's no secret that highly creative teams become more edgy, inspired, and creative over time. They push boundaries and truly innovate.

This is because they feed off each other's creativity, inspire each other, and improve with every project. It's natural to become better at your job when you're doing it to the best of your ability. Most people are ready to contribute given the right set of circumstance. Some may find a good cruising speed. Can you imagine someone like this? Setting the stage for dynamic collaboration will see your team do and be more, sooner.

If you're going to move from static to dynamic collaboration, you'll need to gain greater creative control over your teams and over your own leadership style. This will be a completely new way to express themselves, and it will take practice. Once the magic kicks in, though, you'll see its effects immediately.

Why Greater Creative Control Is Best

When you invest money, time, and effort into giving your team greater creative control of your projects, something incredible happens. Productivity increases, quality of work improves, and the ideas that you base your work on become excellent. Why is this? I believe it's because we return the responsibility for the work back to the creator.

Over the last hundred years, businesses have evolved into many different styles and environments. One hundred years ago was the progressive era, which included reform in many aspects of life. Very few labor unions existed, but child labor was removed (again) and most urban jobs were in crowded factories. The working conditions for the middle class were poor. People were under-paid and most had no benefits. There was no Occupational Safety and Health Act (until 1970). Working conditions, however, were improving from this point and slowly progressing. One main goal of the Progressive movement was the purification of government[4], as Progressives tried to eliminate corruption by exposing and undercutting political machines and bosses. Another fascinating fact of this time was the effects of an Efficiency movement. It was a time for identifying old ways that needed modernizing that brought to bear new scientific, medical, and engineering solutions.

Today, knowledge workers are replacing factory laborers around the world. Our mode moved from production requirements to a substantive measurement. Tools, environment, location, and centralized versus decentralized all have impacted today's employees. This has evolved to new expectations for new ideas, products, and process that have led to pressures on the knowledge workers to innovate or contribute or become irrelevant.

Benefits, rewards, titles, and accolades are all commonplace now in today's innovative environments. Knowing the right amount of each to increase the desire factor for every employee is a difficult effort to calibrate. Some use unique rewards or any

---

4   Progressive Era. *Wikipedia, the free encyclopedia.* http://en.wikipedia.org/wiki/Progressive_Era

highly valued benefits to create an environment of high-level achievers.

I like the implications of combining ownership with responsibilities to create an environment of person pressure or desire to succeed. Netflix, the movie distribution company, has no vacation policy. That does not mean that an employee does not get vacation time. Employees can have as many vacation days as they "feel" they need. However, peer pressure and personal integrity does play a role here. Netflix is very demanding of its employees. The company pays their people well, gives them unlimited vacations, and lets them structure their own compensation packages. In return, high performance is expected. Reed Hastings, the founder, calls this approach "freedom and responsibility."[5] Employees are given the flexibility to do what they do best. The catch is when employees don't live up to expectations, they get "a generous severance package." All this adds to a highly talented and motivated workforce that Netflix will need to survive with tough competitors such as Apple and Amazon in the battle for online movie distribution.

Measurements of success, competencies, and contribution are as necessary as intrinsic values to the organization. Knowing who provides the most value to a company can be skewed. A good political player, a charmer, can survive even though their specific contribution is not measureable. This fits into the category of effective ownership at all levels of the company.

It can be difficult to find the right incentive structures that fit your environment. It is hard to let go of the reins and allow your employees full responsibilities for their non-performance and performance expectations. You must let go and allow your

---

5   Conlin, Michelle. "Netflix: Flex to the Max," Bloomberg Business Week, September 24, 2007. <http://www.businessweek.com/magazine/content/07_39/b4051059.htm>

teams the chance to prove themselves and to blossom. In the beginning, I struggled to relinquish control and trust in the ideas and processes of my team. In the end, when I was able to step back and let them create, that's when the best work was produced. You really can't argue with that!

TRUST IS THE FOUNDATION OF CREATIVE CONTROL...

Businesses want to trust their employees, and they generally want them to care about their business as much as they do. However, with a rapidly changing and migrating employment force, this is hard to accomplish. I had a product development team that I worked with for three years, and they functioned at their best when I was contributing ideas, leaving the team to produce and control the efforts on their own. I should have just left the room.

I was surprised to find that four people in particular seemed to produce outstanding work when I allowed them to brainstorm, chat, and seize total creative control of the project. It took a lot of trust and a few missed deadlines to get it right, but the results were always incredible. Try handing the responsibility back to your employees, do not get involved, and see what evolves—it works!

Trust Improves High Performance

Trust is a major factor in unleashing the creative environment. Both employee and management need to establish an environment of trust. Perhaps that is Netflix's objective in giving employees control over their entire benefit package? The biggest question on building trust is asking where do I focus that relationship in building trust? Is it employee benefit packages, open product development, ownership of all problems within their reach to control and solve?

I have found that "outcomes" are the place to focus. Once expectations of outcomes are understood, all levels of employees understand the mutual relationship of trust. Within the environment of shared ideas and knowledge, we start to accept the fact that we all win. I know the tech industry and what motivates most programmers and development professionals. They are not intimidated by challenges. In fact, they perform best when given a meaty problem to solve. Most do not mind the collaboration or mind-share elements that best solve a logic issue. The chance to learn and grow their knowledge base is what most look for in employment. There are some, however, that work best alone or like to shield their knowledge. Perhaps it is a means of control or protection of their self-worth. Either way, this behavior creates walls and prevents building trust among co-workers.

To mutually reinforce shared experiences and knowledge at every level of the work environment is a factor that takes practice and can be best reflected by management through transparency and engagement. Setting the stage for clear and concise expectations, without fear but instead accountability, always wins trust.

Creativity: Currency of the Future

Because of the technology boom, we've seen a 360 turnaround in what matters in business and what doesn't. Truly, what matters most these days is idea generation. Creativity, in all of its forms, is the currency of the future. The better your creative team, the more successful your projects will be. Technology companies have proven this again and again.

A single great idea can mean billions. Several good ideas can mean the same. Whatever is happening in the world of business right now, heed this warning: start building up your creative potential because it's going to be worth more than all the other assets combined.

The early introduction of venture capitalists[6] into the technology sector in the early 1950s by George Doriot, known as the "father of venture capitalism," the former dean of Harvard Business School and founder of American Research & Development Corporation (ARDC), with Ralph Flanders and Karl Compton, former president of MIT, worked to encourage private investments in veteran-owned businesses after World War II. Their first big success was $70,000 in a company called Digital Equipment Corporation (DEC) in 1957, turning their investment into a 500 times return. This was the start of building wealth by connecting investment capital to smart people. Without venture capital, Silicon Valley would not have existed. It's the relationship between investment and those ideas from the likes of Fairchild Semiconductor, Tandem, Atari, Cisco, Genentech, and Apple that led to a new revolution, a digital revolution that I and millions of others still live and love.

Creativity is a commodity and extremely valuable to the entire economic system. The world is putting an increasingly high value on creativity talent and well-executed ideas. Originality, flexibility, testing, and aligning your brand with a specific product is becoming very important indeed. Google is known for their search engine. Samsung is making waves in the smartphone industry.

Every successful tech company in the world has invested small fortunes in gaining the best and brightest creative talent they can find. It's why you hear about talent poaching so often in the tech field. CEO X has moved over to company B and is

---

6   History of private equity and venture capital. *Wikipedia, the free encyclopedia.* <http://en.wikipedia.org/wiki/History_of_private_equity_and_venture_capital>

now acting president. It's all about WHO is in your business now, not what your business puts out.

This is why creativity is the currency of the future. People will become the major assets of a company due to their ability to come up with excellent ideas. I think I can safely say that the employees that are truly gifted creatively will become the managers and leaders of the future. They will ensure that the products their company creates are the best.

Even now, progressive thinkers such as Rodney Hill are questioning the current education models and calling for systems of learning that harness creative talent. There is a great need in the world for creative ability or the ability to bring order out of chaos. We'll need it going forward to solve problems such as climate change, overpopulation, and food shortages.

The creative workforce will be the big players in securing the future for companies all over the world. Cultivating that workforce to believe in its capabilities will be the driving force to solid human asset management. Without innovation, creation, and originality, many new businesses will fail. Creativity is currency and secures differentiation and employment for those that have it and can call to it on cue. When recruiters look at resumes, they are not only looking at experience so much as portfolios, or the applicant's ability to create. We spend our entire careers gaining experience that we never truly use for anyone's benefit. Think about it! Wouldn't it make more sense to improve the creativity skill?

There are too many barriers that are placed in front of creative people just because of out-dated rules. Who cares if a person only has four years of experience instead of ten? Does this mean they won't be able to do a great job? No! Essentially, it all comes down to their level of creativity and how well they've used it over the years.

Gaining the Competitive Edge with CE 2.0

As senior executives, we have all heard and used the term "competitive edge." This term, sometimes overused, suggests we have the ability to execute or act on it. But what is it and how do we measure it? Do we always have it when we say we do?

This is why I have introduced CE 2.0. CE 2.0 is real, accountable, and action-oriented. It embodies the deep understanding of the competitive environment compared to the asset management of your product innovation activities.

Business analysts are now saying that creativity is the new competitive advantage, and they're right. It's no longer the collective experience of your team that makes it valuable, but the creations that they are able to devise and launch into the market. Creative potential is so much more important than any other human trait.

The Traitorous Eight[7] were highly capable innovators who left Shockley Semiconductor Laboratory in 1957 due to conflicts with William Shockley, a Nobel Laureate in physics, but terrible manager. The next day they signed a contract for $1.3 million with a New York firm called Fairchild Camera and Instruments, which was involved with missiles and satellite systems. The eight men were: Julius Blank, Victor Grinich, Jean Hoerni, Gene Kleiner, Jay Last, Gordon Moore, Robert Noyce, and Sheldon Roberts. Most know what happened next; that Fairchild Semiconductor became the largest technology enterprise with many organizational changes since. But, due to the Traitorous Eight's sheer knowledge base, the team gained funding before private or venture foundering was even available. Creativity, confidence, and perhaps timing are great partners. We can all use a little of the latter.

---

7   The Traitorous Eight Traitorously Leave Shockley Semiconductor
<http://www.pbs.org/transistor/album1/eight/index.html>

A 2010 Ernst and Young study concluded that "the ability to manage, organize, cultivate and nurture creative thinking is directly linked to growth and achievement."

The competitive edge is a visual perspective that needs to be turned into reality. Creative control of the innovation asset takes practice and focus. When a senior manager starts the strategic process of planning how to overtake or become better than its competitors, there are several things to consider:

1. How well do you know my competitor's market advantage?
2. Is their market advantage tied to the human asset or management style?
3. How different is their management team and staff from yours?
4. Is it just about company size or product differentiation?
5. Can one new invention or product be the game changer?

My guess is you are closer to overtaking your competitors then you think! A recalibration to a more focused innovation environment will get you there. CE 2.0 demands that you focus closer on one or two innovations that will push your firm ahead of the sector you serve.

CE 2.0 Case in Point – The mileage reward industry is very competitive. Credit card companies, airlines, and merchants all work together to build top of mind brand commitment in the minds of the consumer. One company, a boutique loyalty agency in Zurich, Switzerland, is a small fraction of the size of the biggest loyalty agencies operating today's highly competitive reward industry.

Before starting Loylogic with his business partners Bruno Frieden and Thomas Kindler in 2005, Dominic Hofer, CEO, discovered that his demanding personality did not fit in a conventional corporate setting. *"I felt the need to create, compete, and the demand for those around me to inspire and contribute quickly. I have high expectations for others and myself. That can be a bit conflictive if I am not the person in charge,"* Dominic states.

That drive to rise to the top of the industry is probably why Loylogic has claimed the prestigious Swiss Economic Award for rapid growth through innovation. *"The point-based loyalty industry is a very competitive business and is driven by new methods and innovation. We are faced with the same hurdle that large companies are faced with except we have very limited resources. It is our passion to serve our clients and stay in business that keeps us driven."*

When asked what his formula is for inspiring the 100 creative team members at Loylogic, Dominic claims, *"It lies in urgency. I sleep very little each night, maybe three hours, mostly due to my enthusiasm and passion for the business. My staff mirrors this as they see that I am willing to go the extra limits. This seems to create a self-calibration for my team and their willingness to contribute. We align and adjust together."*

Besides winning new business on a grand scale with the likes of American Express Global, Loylogic has matched the technical sophistication of Google with their mobile currency point wallet launched in September 2012. According to Dominic, *"PointsPay shows the dream growth curves that every small business venture strives for. We brought a disruptive mobile technology to market and a solution that responds to a decade-old need of loyalty program members worldwide: redeeming miles and points everywhere users shop. After investing two years in developing PointsPay, we are very pleased with the outcome. We are not the size of Google but seem to be able to innovate at that scale."* Today PointsPay has already achieved strong global coverage and continues to grow at a 47% monthly rate.

The focus that Loylogic committed to in the beginning of their innovation strategy resulted in a major differentiating factor. Without the team passion, vision, and commitment to their strategic milestones, they could not have accomplished a feat similar to that of a Google proportion.

Education vs. Practical Application

I touched on this in the previous section, but it really warrants further discussion for these reasons:

- Firstly, you need to know how to hire people in your company.
- Secondly, you need to focus on building a strong creative team.
- Finally, team members that can visualize and DO are more valuable than those with fancy degrees and years of experience.

The biggest hiring mistake that you can make these days is to hire people just because they look good on paper. An impressive degree does not mean the person is as good as the credentials may suggest. It certainly makes the hiring process more complex. You have to work a little harder for evidence of creativity and actual accomplishments in innovation.

But all good managers and business owners will take the time to do this. If they want to build their creative human capital and be competitive, then that's what they're looking for on resumes. Education is just not as essential anymore. When a 12-year-old kid in Bangalore, India, can teach himself seven programming languages like a 45-year-old veteran at Microsoft, you have to wonder! And yes, this happens every day around the world.

People are advancing, skills are becoming bigger and better, and people are teaching themselves to be great. So when you compare two resumes, think about this—will the highly educated person be able to produce the goods? You already know that the practical person can, because it's all there in their resume.

I ONCE HAD TO DECIDE BETWEEN TWO PEOPLE WHO APPLIED FOR THE SAME POSITION...

An educated junior manager with a degree in business science and marketing and five years' experience or one without a degree who managed to create a Top 20 app at the Apple iTunes store and kept it there for three months. While the educated person seemed like the obvious choice, I just couldn't hire her.

The real decision came at the face-to-face interview. The second person spoke enthusiastically about her passion for coding and how badly she wanted to prove herself in a corporate environment. The educated woman kept recounting template answers like they were from an interview book. I hired the proven entity.

You see, practical application is counting for more and more in the business world. It's nearly necessary to be educated, of course, but it says nothing about your capability level. The creativity you had when you entered college is at the same level when you graduate. Proven innovators, on the other hand, constantly expand their creativity, because they are bursting with ideas.

If you can find a born creator, someone who finds and spreads joy whenever they are charged with making something new and innovative—grab them! They are rare. And believe me, they are worth more to you and your business than a highly educated person that will never have the same creative drive or passion.

It makes sense then to say that you need to re-organize your hiring processes to get more applicable people on your team.

If creativity is the goal, then your company is lagging behind. Stop aiming for education and start aiming for application!

Commodities and Creativity

In this 21st century that we live in, creativity is the top commodity, and you should be restructuring your business accordingly. Promoting people based on years with the company, projects done, and money earned is not valid anymore. Instead, if you see a dynamic creator, promote them to inspire others.

Make "incredibly creative" the desired norm. That means transforming your business into a creative hub that will not only attract the right people, but keep them there—doing their best work for you. That's essentially what the best tech companies do. Look at Google for example. It's an honor to work for Google, even though the pay may be lower than Microsoft. This is because Google makes it notoriously hard to become part of their staff, and they promote a highly creative work environment.

How can you make your business attractive to top creative commodities? It's time you begin thinking about that. There will be many other creative-based businesses out there soon, and they will certainly be thinking about what makes them the better business to apply to.

Soon the creative model will become a matter of survival for your business, not just a means to be more successful. In this uncertain time of economic turmoil, change, and unstable financial systems, it's creativity that will rise as the new desirable skill set that everybody wants. Creativity will become your number one strategic priority in the future.

Don't think of creativity as an artist painting or a writer writing —it's so much more than that. Creativity is about creation. Every job position needs to be moved forward or needs to progress in order to succeed. You need ALL of your employees to be creative so that they can handle this responsibility.

They have to come up with good solutions to nagging problems. An accountant, for example, might get a new piece of software developed that saves the company time and human resources each month when sorting out the checks and balances. Whatever the role, creativity will be the commodity.

It's not just creativity in general but individual creativity and team-based creativity that will catapult your business into the big leagues. According to Baer and Oldham, *"Considerable evidence now suggests that employee creativity can make a substantial contribution to an organization's growth and competitiveness."*

Innovation can be responsible for unlimited future income, as long as you can guarantee the creative input. That means investing heavily in creative resources right now and training highly creative teams to come up with products and solutions that will put your business on the map now and in the future.

CHAPTER 7

The Anatomy of an Idea

"Nearly every man who develops an idea works it up to the point where it looks impossible, and then he gets discouraged. That's not the place to become discouraged."

THOMAS EDISON

Ideas are the small building blocks of creativity. The creative process itself consists of many ideas or a combination of ideas from different sources. My mother was an artist and preferred to call herself one, even though she worked as a quality control inspector for LL Bean in Freeport, Maine, most of her career.

As an artist, her creative inspiration would strike her at two in the morning, and she would sacrifice sleep to indulge in the idea process when it inspired her. Her works of art would be stacked everywhere, and many were incomplete. According to her, one painting would inspire her to start another. Eventually, she would return and finish them, maybe not the year started, but eventually they all would be part of her final inspiration. It was an incredible organic process that never seemed to end. It was her system, and it worked well for her.

Vincent Van Gogh once said, *"Great things are not done by impulse, but by a series of small things brought together."* I believe my mother found joy in her ideas, and the act of creation was secondary to them.

The Creative Lifecycle (Concept, Elaboration, Accommodation)

The creative lifecycle is ever-changing and yet it involves many common features that can be analyzed and studied so that we can better understand how it works. Defined, creativity is the generation of ideas that are useful or novel. But ideas are only part of the process. If they aren't used to create something in the physical world, you can't call it creativity.

In a way, you could say that coming up with ideas is central to creativity, which is why it's important to understand how people collectively and individually produce them. The creative lifecycle begins with three basic steps. These steps prepare the creator for the creative process and help them to execute it efficiently.

Far from being unexplainable and mysterious, these steps involve concept formulation, elaboration, and, finally, accommodation. As the creator moves through each phase of the creative lifecycle, something goes from being an idea to being a tangible thing.

- **Conception:** Developing concepts outside of the norm that may be included or represented are all part of the creative cycle. For example, Netflix has a very innovative business model that began as an idea and became a concept—the concept of never having to pay late fees for rented movies ever again! This conception phase includes looking at your average business model and integrating this with your new concept idea.

- **Elaboration:** Once new concepts have been pinned down, these have to be added to the original problem representation. In other words, the concept needs to be elaborated on, explored, and analyzed. Many unforeseen issues can arise at this stage if all angles aren't covered. For example, there would be new revenue streams for Netflix because of the Internet, BUT they may lose money from not having any brick-and-mortar stores.

- **Accommodation:** When the problem has been restructured and the processes of conception and elaboration complete, the final phase is accommodation. This is when the developed idea is applied to the larger issue. In Netflix's case, they had to focus on the issue of providing streaming movies to people.

Search, Mixing, Insight, and Reinterpretation

In the creative process, there are four common intuitions that experts use to explain creative results. They are search, mixing, insight, and reinterpretation. If your team is looking for a way to express themselves creatively more often, this is great to know. However, while tried and true, be careful to recognize time wasting patterns when the outcomes are not genuine (discussed in chapter 9).

While these are all true, they are not all required for creative productivity to take place. These definitions help us understand how creative people work, but they don't explain why some people are better at this than others or HOW we can replicate it to inspire more creativity in less-creative people.

1. Creative ideas come from searching, or from "unexplored" possibilities.

2. Creative ideas come from mixing new and old methods or results.

3. Creative ideas come from sudden moments of insight.

4. Creative ideas come from reinterpretations of conventional thinking.

What I do know is that if you want to become a manager who can handle the creative control of a company, you need to find people that have the will to innovate—and then work with them to unleash larger amounts of their creative core talent.

- ***Improve search talent.*** If you can teach your teams how to actively search for solutions to problems—for things that inspire or stimulate—then you can help them improve a key step in the creative lifecycle. Creative people tend to search in unusual places, thinking outside the box to gain new perspectives.

- ***Improve the ability to mix ideas.*** Get your team together and mix their knowledge in order to yield more creative ideas. The simple act of discussing search results in a group can lead to greater findings, new ideas, and the generation of unique concepts.

- ***Improve the way you reinterpret information.*** Creative is about changing how you think in different contexts—meaning that you reframe problems in new ways to find uncommon solutions. Meet the problem with "new eyes" and redefine goals, elements, and actions in a project.

- *Improve how your team is inspired.* Moments of insight come when creative people have been stimulated, motivated, and inspired to do better. These clear moments can change the course of entire projects. Sudden insight is an important step in the creative process, but it can't be forced. These moments happen unexpectedly, at times of heightened communication or introspection.

Using Your Team to Find Answers or Ideas

The first step in helping your company improve its creative process involves getting them to find answers or ideas by searching for them when they are needed most. In this process, there are three kinds of main information that your team will be looking for: goals, elements, and actions.

If your problem, for example, is to remove all legacy programming from the business, there are working parts that you'll need to figure out in order to do this. The goal is your completed vision for what that should be replaced with. The elements involved will be your understanding of how to use the team and other resources within your company.

Finally, your actions will involve which tools you need to use and how to use them to the benefit of your project. To find innovative solutions, you will need to source the stakeholders and measure up against expectations to devise your ultimate plan of action.

You will then apply this newfound knowledge of information to the problem representation elements. If you've done a proper search and discovered the answers, your output will meet your goals or expectations for the project.

Keep in mind that there are two types of searches that can be conducted here. A habitual search is not going to get you the same results as an uncommon search. These habitual searches result in non-creative outcomes and don't support the creative process. Another way of seeing it is to identify the difference between routine and non-routine searches.

A search that you might conduct in general won't spark that creativity needed to formulate the solutions needed to solve your core problem. Sure, they might help clarify a few things, but overall what you need are "unusual" searches—or creative searches that don't follow your average thought patterns.

If you can take charge and teach your team what the difference is between routine and non-routine searching in the creative process, you could prepare them to be better team members, who contribute more to the group problem.

Search can sometimes be like heading into a maze. There are thousands of potential directions you could choose, many of which may lead to the exit. During your search, you'll test out different passage combos and directions. Eventually you'll forge a new exit for yourself, and an end to the problem.

Routine thinking may have you trying to locate an exit, while non-routine thinking will have you build your own exit at a more interesting part of the maze. This, in concept, is the difference between habitual and uncommon searches. Anyone can learn what this part of the process means and how to use it to sharpen their overall goals.

The most creative people don't see walls when they are trying to build a house. They see opportunities and potential. If you keep hitting walls, your limitations will box you in and hold you back. Then you can only follow the prescribed building rules. A famous architect, Samuel Mockbee, won numerous awards for building houses out of tires, hay, and other found items.

This completely non-traditional outcome was fuelled by his ability to use non-routine search practices to think along new and exciting paths. If he was thinking like everyone else and building homes out of brick and wood, he may never have won those awards.

How to Mix These Ideas Together

Ideas can be great on their own, as many are, but in a team environment, you'd be silly not to combine the creative potential of all the minds in the room and share their ideas with each other. Everyone has a different perspective or viewpoint that they use to come up with solutions to project problems.

The more people you can involve in the idea-mixing process, the better your potential outcomes will be for your project. Mixing is a great way to change the problem representation and to get to the bottom of new ideas.

I like to have open brainstorming sessions with my teams, where everyone has a turn to offer their perspectives and searches on a project. One by one, people go around and say their piece while everyone else takes notes. Once everyone is finished, there is a discussion about potential improvements or new ideas.

SOMETIMES MIXED IDEAS WORK AND SOMETIMES THEY DON'T...

As the manager in charge of this creative control process, it's up to you to decide what does and doesn't work. Think of ideas as different kinds of drink mixes. Sodas go well with orange juice, but not all sodas. You can mix together rum and coke, for example, but not milk and coke.

There will always be exceptions to the rule, and as the manager, it will be your job to steer your team in the right direction. That means supporting great ideas and guiding the conversation sometimes to produce the right outcomes.

The mixing process doesn't give people license to freely combine any and all ideas. That's not what the creative process is about. Along with the entire abstract, there is also a real sense of control and what will work well together.

New ideas aren't hard to come by using these methods, but really great ideas are. But you can't predict the quality of the mix. I've had teams propose ideas to each other and absolutely no fresh ideas resulted from it.

I've also had teams share ideas and then suddenly experience a massive boom in creativity, which leads to excellent ideas for the project. Keep in mind that mixing is not a sure-thing process —it can be very inefficient and takes a lot of trial and error to get right.

If your teams are struggling to combine their ideas into something great, take a look at the team. Either they have not conducted their original search process along uncommon lines or they just aren't finding synergy with their other team members. To correct this problem, you can always try bringing someone new onto the team.

Often a fresh perspective can change the course of a project. Because you're relying on people to naturally combine their project ideas into something excellent, you'll need to introduce fresh ideas into the mix if the existing ideas aren't gelling well together.

Increase your "hit rate" by building strong teams that work well with each and are able to effectively share in a working environment. When people have good chemistry, then their ideas often have good chemistry. Work on this to get the most out of your teams.

Using Insight to Streamline Your Dominant Idea

Insight is the one intuition that has been measured and found to be a must-have feature in the creative lifecycle process. Yet no one knows how or why it happens; it just does. These "eureka" moments can be responsible for restricting project outcomes.

For centuries experts and people of note have spoken about the creative process as being heavily linked to moments of insight or a single moment of insight. This can happen at any time during the creation process—and it usually comes from one particular person.

You can use this incredible insight to streamline your dominant idea. Often it's these moments that shed light on an area of a project that needed some tweaking. Suddenly, in a "eureka" moment, the problem will just solve itself, or the solution will be obvious.

Insight into a project can take time, as experts have discovered. It's more likely for these moments of insight to happen after a project idea has been thought about for a fair amount of time. That's why you can't rush creativity—it happens when it wants to!

Kepler, for example, reinterpreted planetary motion, but it took him six years to do that after he realized that predictions using circular orbits didn't match observations. If you want to integrate this important step of the creative lifecycle into a working environment, then I would suggest always allowing your team time to really think about your chosen ideas.

As a manager that is looking to exert creative control over their team, it's imperative that you try to promote a team environment where everyone understands their role and takes an active interest in everyone else's roles as well. This total understanding of a project allows people to better understand the working parts of the process.

At this point, they have a better frame of reference, and insights will come a lot easier to them. At work, most problems that are proposed to teams are non-linear problems in that they have no pre-existing or easy answers. This means your team can't use their long-term memory functions to solve these issues.

They need to tap into their working memory and find answers based on their creative potential. Working memory is great for solving complex issues, but using it often will also lead to more "aha!" moments. They will come at random times—during a shower or while sleeping or eating—but they will come.

Insight can really take a good project and make it a great one. Once you have targeted what your core ideas will be, you'll need to activate that working memory of yours to solve the finer problems of the project to make everything viable.

This means promoting the elements that inspire insightful thinking. Quiet places, inward-looking, not actively trying to solve the issue and being a bit happy have all been found to improve a person's ability to be insightful.

Reinterpreting the Idea

When something is reinterpreted, it is seen in a totally new light. One of the most important factors of the creative lifecycle is understanding how this reinterpretation affects the idea generation process.

Seeing an old problem with new eyes, as it's called, is a creative technique that has been used for centuries. It involves stepping back and taking the time to consider in new ways a problem that you have been obsessing about.

You have to adapt the problem-solving model as a starting point if you're ever going to solve a really tough issue. To do this, you need to reconsider the role of goals, elements, and actions in your thought processes.

It's not easy changing the way you think about something and disturbing your natural cognitive processes. But this is

BOB COULDN'T FIGURE OUT HOW TO MAKE THIS ONE BIT OF CODE WORK...

And it was centered on a really innovative piece of design that was set to launch in less than a month. After searching, mixing, and repeatedly discussing this portion of the project, it was clear that this issue had no real solution.

So, my team leader took a step back from the project and focused on other things for a while. He began to see the problem in new ways, after being influenced by the other work that he was doing, and eventually discovered the solution on his own. This is exactly what reinterpreting the idea is all about.

essential if you're going to apply the appropriate amount of creativity to any project. ALL creative projects hit walls that need to be torn down.

The final step in this phase will always be to see things with new or fresh eyes. That's how you dismiss all the preconceived notions that you had about the problem to start fresh with new perspectives. All great creative people are able to do this.

Thomas Edison, for example, tried to create a decent lightbulb over 1,000 times before getting it right. That means he worked consistently on the same problems for a very long time, re-examining them, learning, and then reframing the problems. Originally, the first light bulbs lasted a mere 150 hours, and then, ten years later, Edison introduced one that lasted 1,200 hours. Today the average light bulb lasts approximately 1,500 hours.

It's only by doing this that he managed to push forward and break through those mental barriers that hold us all back. There are always better solutions to our problems; we just have to find them.

As a creative control leader, it will be your job to get your team to understand the role that reinterpretation plays in the creative lifecycle. When you are aware of it, you are better able to manage it along with the three other core parts: search, mixing, and insight.

These are the basic moving parts involved in the anatomy of ideas. One or many ideas make up the creative process, so it makes sense that to improve creativity in your teams, you should also try to improve these intuitive elements.

CHAPTER 8

Overcoming Social Suppression

"With physical and financial capital having been replaced by human capital as the economy's driving force, the knowledge, skills and experiences of people have become this country's scarce resource."

LOWELL MILKEN

If you asked any financially successful businessperson what the most important secret is for them in building a successful company, they will say one thing—the people they've hired! As technology rises, so does the importance of human capital in business. This makes all the difference!

People have always played a significant role in the success of businesses everywhere, but these days it's so much more than that. Having creative, intelligent, hard-working people in your company is essential. Knowing how and when to inspire the human asset to unleash its full potential all at a high-performance pace is key. Knowing the triggers, the rewards, the environment, the peers, and all the other complex attributes that can encourage or discourage employees are the keys to unlocking those complex people.

Suppression of one's involvement is an area that must be considered if you wish to understand the full scope of your innovation assets. Suppression is defined as the conscious decision to delay the consideration of circumstances.

For example, issues such as hurt feelings, bullying, personal events, domineering participants, sexual harassment, shyness, bad performance reviews, office romances, over-excitement, difficult expectations, unclear expectations, anxieties, lack of sleep, and other distractions can be reasons for suppressing involvement or participation and can have a negative impact on your performance.

The role emotions can have on our overall individual performance is strong and can directly affect the dynamics of teams and groups, ultimately impacting revenue. There are over 600 words in English that describe emotions and 43 facial muscles to express them physically. Even though there are over 6,000 languages[8] in the world, most have no trouble figuring if someone is registering happiness, surprise, or disgust by just looking at a person's face. And with that understanding, we can, within reason, evaluate our own emotions, interpret them, and determine which emotions we will choose to react to them.

We can control our own emotions as well as the effects that other people's emotions may have on us. The paradox lies in understanding the triggers of stronger emotions in us and how what we show impacts others. There is an immediate relationship that forms as soon as we walk into a meeting or conference call or send an email that may impact the symbiotic relationship between parties.

---

8   Emotions in the workplace. *Wikipedia, the free encyclopedia*
http://en.wikipedia.org/wiki/Emotions_in_the_workplace

The important part of this lesson is recognizing oneself and one's impact on the team and, as a manager, effectively becoming a master at determining how best to create an environment that reduces reason for suppressing contributions.

Social suppression can also affect perception. If I am thinking about one thing, studying one subject, or expecting an outcome, I may be so focused, or distracted, that I may miss a very important opportunity in front of me. Have I suppressed my scope of vision, aptitude, or expectations? If I am not fully aware of unlimited opportunities and have the desire to be open to the unexpected, I am missing something that could have a dramatic effect for my company.

In 1928, Scottish scientist Sir Alexander Fleming[9] was studying Staphylococcus—the bacteria that causes food poisoning. He turned up at work one day and discovered a blue-green mold that seemed to be inhibiting growth of the bacteria. He grew a pure culture of the mold and discovered that it was a Penicillium mold. After further experiments, Fleming was convinced that penicillin would not last long enough in the human body to kill pathogenic bacteria, thus he stopped studying it after 1931. It was not until 1934 that he restarted some clinical trials and continued to try to get someone to purify it until 1940. The development of penicillin for use as a medicine is attributed to the Australian Nobel Laureate Howard Walter Florey; he shared the Nobel Prize with Fleming and Ernst Boris Chain.

Percy LeBaron Spencer[10] of the Raytheon Company was walking past a radar tube, and he noticed that the chocolate bar in his pocket melted. He later returned with some corn kernels,

9   Bellis, Mary. The History of Penicillin. *About.com Guide*. <http://inventors.about.com/od/pstartinventions/a/Penicillin.htm>

10 Fascinating facts about Percy Lebaron Spencer. *The Great Idea Finder*. <http://www.ideafinder.com/history/inventors/spencer.htm>

placed it in front of the magnetron, and watched the corn pop all over the floor. This became our highly used microwave oven.

There are numerous examples like these that would not have found themselves in our lives had not the inventor been open-minded to the possibilities.

Your Main Corporate Asset – Innovation

For many years, the economy has been organized around mass production, quantity over quality, and churning out goods to make the most money. This was the old model that was highly successful at making business owners small fortunes.

But these days, this process simply doesn't work—especially in the tech field. When the work that is being done is highly reliant on skill, intelligence, and creativity, you can't focus on churning ideas out, mass producing ideas, or selling ideas to make more ideas.

Instead, businesses have had to change their focus completely. We now rely on the talents of individuals to keep our company going. In the past decade, I've seen young, inexperienced people come up with one solid idea and earn millions from it.

HEADHUNTING HAS RECENTLY BECOME A SERIOUS BUSINESS...

With companies scrambling to secure the best and brightest for their own teams. There is no denying that a single person with a great idea is worth an absolute fortune in the technology niche.

Even better is a team of people that can come up with incredible ideas for the market, based on teamwork. Never underestimate the creative talent of an individual; they could end up changing your entire business.

Instagram, for example, was created in someone's garage. It was a very good idea for image editing that was proliferated by one or two people. Shortly after being created and used, Instagram was sold to Facebook for $1 billion.

Needless to say, it is people that are your most valuable asset. Those with the best teams and most innovations aren't affected by economic turndowns or dips in sales. Instead, their people keep them going with a never-ending supply of fresh ideas, incredible creativity, and hugely innovative products.

The conceptual means for developing ideas and innovation does not happen in a vacuum. It is nurtured and coddled. It is the most important asset, which needs and deserves respect. We need to agree that the creative process should mean everything to your company. Therefore it requires more emphasis—so everyone in your company understands its importance and their contribution to it.

The Human Investment

I have a cousin who is a retired United States Air Force Lieutenant Colonel. His last job before retiring was supporting NASA as a Space Shuttle Contingency Operations and Training Officer. His job was to prepare on-scene commanders and their response forces to properly react to an unscheduled emergency landing of the Space Shuttle Orbiter Vehicle at designated contingency landing sites around the world. All phases of space shuttle missions were supported to include: launch, on-orbit and scheduled end-of-mission. This has always been my favorite case analogy for contingency strategy. We all need a contingency plan that allows us alternative landing sites, regardless of the strategy or tactic initiated.

When we invest in the human asset, we are investing in unlimited possibilities. One employee can become as good as three. Or one employee could be the catalyst for the next big thing in the marketplace. This investment in human capital is the most important part of your job; seeking it, protecting it, and cultivating it. I visualize my staff as important as those astronauts working in the space shuttle. Their training, practices, contingency awareness, and their interesting and not so interesting work that gets performed are just as important as your team's duties. This visualization is real, and those assets sitting at desks, computers, and whiteboards are the best of the best. If you treat them as such, they will perform!

Pre-digital days, finding good people for your company was relatively easy. You'd already have a reputation locally, and placing an ad in the paper was enough to get people to send in their resumes in the hope of securing a job at your company.

Today things are far more complicated. Job seekers have hundreds of choices when they're looking for a job, locally or internationally. They consider factors like "benefits," "salary," "career expansion," "business culture," "location," "peers," "financial performance," and how it may stack up against one of your competitors.

The best job seekers have usually spent money on education and are looking to join a leading company where they can make a difference. In fact, the better the job seeker is at what they do, the more in demand they will be. It also makes them far harder to secure.

Tech companies compete with the biggest and the best in the world right now. These tech companies are expected to have the latest technologies and the most attractive work–life balance.

In order to stay on top of what is increasingly becoming a global economy, businesses need to place more emphasis on developing and retaining people. In the past, attitudes, abilities, and skills were seen as paramount to productivity and organizational performance. Now, as we begin to understand creativity more, this has taken precedence.

In fact, it's not wrong to say that creativity has become a two-way street for business and potential employees. Companies want very creative, motivated people, and the potential employee wants a job where they can express their creativity and be on the cutting edge of their field. This is often the goal for motivated people working in the tech niche.

It's your job as the innovation officer to get your company to realize how important hiring great people can be for your business. The human investment is important for these reasons:

- They rapidly improve your creative potential and motivate others.
- They help make your company invulnerable to economic instability.
- They guarantee the future success of new product releases.

It's a well-known fact that large companies struggle to keep their best people. There's a good reason for this—large companies don't give their employees what they deserve. Understanding how to treat your employees is the first step to retaining a competent, highly-creative workforce.

If you can secure some truly innovative people by spending a bit extra or by changing your hiring process, then you'll be on track for great things really soon. It's all about context and perspective.

Money and Creativity

Money tends to follow creativity around. Companies are becoming better at identifying who their key assets are, and they pay them accordingly. Worse yet are the head hunters that steal great people from your company.

They are asked to offer your best people more money to change jobs. A lot of the time, more money is enough to convince someone to change where they work. Because corporations have inspired a culture that makes people feel insignificant—like cogs in a machine—people tend to have very little loyalty for the companies they work for.

They will almost always go where the money is. You can't blame them! While some people believe that money shouldn't be the only factor involved in deciding where they work, it's the strongest factor. You have to come to terms with the reality that when you offer more money to the right people, that can change your entire business. Hiring and keeping innovators is the greatest investment you can make as long as it makes sense. Not all people are the same; there are different levels of performance values, and everyone, all the time, has to prove themselves.

Differentiation through Creative Incentive Programs

One of the greatest ways to start the positive information flow about your company and setting the tone as a company that cares about its creative assets, the people, is to offer a compensation plan that they feel they are part of. Earlier, I used Netflix as an example for creative compensation packages. Not all companies are the size or location or in the same sector as Netflix, so it may not work to emulate their program. I am suggesting a program that combines both choice and incentives, driven by an employee's need to build the program that kicks in their highest degree of desire to excel.

** The following are offered as examples for you to change and adapt to your specific needs, circumstance, and environment. The object is to improve ownership by an employee with a level of risk-reward attached to their salary. This will sort out those people who are confident in their ability to contribute versus those that are not willing to value their output on a performance based structure:

Incentive Structure 1 (potential for 25% over Pure Base Compensation)

50% Base Pay combined with 50% Regular Performance Incentives

Incentives Base on a scale from 3–15% of base; they are rewarded on:

- Project Completion
- Meeting Team Objectives
- Product Development Milestones
- Code Quality
- Corporate Lifestyle Contribution
- Innovation Patents
- Exercise Milestones

Employees will set their own incentive targets.

Incentive Structure 2 (potential for 15% over Pure Base Compensation)

75% Base Pay combined with 25% Performance Incentives

Incentives Base on a scale from 3–10% of base; they are rewarded on:

- Project Completion
- Meeting Team Objectives
- Product Development Milestones
- Code Quality
- Corporate Lifestyle Contribution
- Innovation Patents
- Exercise Milestones

Employees will set their own incentive targets.

Incentive Structure 3

100% Pure Base Pay

Employee 360 Evaluation Performance Program:

- Project Completion
- Meeting Team Objectives
- Product Development Milestones
- Code Quality
- Corporate Lifestyle Contribution
- Innovation Patents

Their peers will judge the employee's quarterly performance contribution.

CREATIVE PEOPLE MAY BE INNOVATIVE, BUT THEY ARE SHREWD...

I've hired a few individuals who claim to be extraordinary, but I later found out they were not as good in real life as they presented on paper. I've also hired humble people that turned out to be high achievers and contributors but didn't expect a large salary. Most of the time creative people care more about their work contribution, as well as having a keen sense for their true market value.

If you can't offer them something special, then they will look elsewhere—and this could mean losing a team member that has the potential to make your company millions of dollars. You have to assess each person individually, give them the information they need to make a good choice, but more importantly, set the stage for a long and trusted relationship.

The overall objective is to get all employees to see the value of contribution to the overall corporate mission and participate with a desire to increase their earnings while contributing to the overall goodwill of the company community.

The Hindrance of Hierarchies

There are many organizational influences on people within your company, but there is one in particular that tends to hinder creativity of all kinds. I'm talking about hierarchies. While the traditional hierarchies in a company certainly positively impact other organizational goals, they tend to have a negative impact on the structure of creativity:

- Unnecessary bureaucratic layering
- Insignificance of manager's influence on subordinate's work
- Greed and insensitivity
- Not working towards a company goal but personal goals

Creative individuals find that collaboration, integration, and innovation are more conducive to idea generation than work assignment, policing, and following the rules. A hierarchy in a working environment consists of your entry level workers, their bosses, and more bosses—until you go up several levels to reach the management team.

What these structures do is they make the underlings feel insignificant, overworked, stressed, and not very creative, particularly those with career ambitions. In these strict structural settings, the new, younger talent in the lower levels may be hidden from opportunities.

Even if they did have great ideas, working it up the chain of command is a problem. What happens if one of the bosses doesn't like the idea and shuts it down? This can cause problems later on. Eventually the creative and talented subordinate will leave because they feel stifled and pointless in their jobs.

Hierarchies hinder creativity. That's why, instead of focusing on making people follow the rules, you should be encouraging a more open and less restricted work culture. For example, Pixar, the animation company, is dedicated to fostering an environment that promotes trusting and respecting work relationships and unleashes everyone's creativity.

A nice side effect of this business culture is that every truly talented animator that leaves college wants to work at Pixar. Everyone there can come up with ideas or suggest changes to the schedule or work processes.

Is your working environment this open and free? If not, then you need to think about loosening up that stranglehold that you have on your employees. Making people accountable for their work doesn't mean policing them as a boss 24/7. It means trusting them enough to find solutions and to ask for help if they need it.

When creative people feel like they are being monitored or scrutinized, then creativity drops. It's like that with most people. You can't allow hierarchies to get in the way of the creative process.

In your average hierarchal workspace, roles are strictly defined, and rational thinking and decision making are seen as paramount to the daily functions of the business. Relationships are business-like, impersonal, and tense. In a creative environment, there is a sense of belonging to a group or team; people work towards organizational goals, and they are team-orientated.

Creative Suppression through People

How is it possible to suppress creativity? Easy! With other people! The older hierarchical structures that make the workplace so cold and impersonal are natural creativity suppressors. The biggest way a company loses out on creativity is by ignoring how their other employees (especially management) behave with people.

When something hinders creativity, it threatens the power structure in a business. How much more value can a subordinate have than the CEO when that creative subordinate came up with an idea that made the company millions? It's a tough process to change.

You've seen it and maybe even experienced it when people in positions of power hold others back. This is done for many reasons, and I'll name a few here:

- Bosses may feel threatened that subordinates are trying to take their job.
- They don't want to look incompetent in front of their own bosses.
- They don't want the subordinates to get the credit for their idea or the work.
- Bosses feel they should be the ones teaching, not learning.

Old organizational structures replaced uncertainty with routine to maximize predictability and order. This is not the ideal climate for creative people to be in. In fact, you need to implement some kind of training that teaches people in your company the difference between hierarchal organizations and creative environments.

There needs to be less emphasis on job descriptions and power struggles. Rules and regulations need to be toned down to reduce conservative thinking. There needs to be a system in place that your company uses to reward people whose behavior results in creative products.

Most of all, hierarchy violations really need to be eliminated. It's important to have a boss, yes, but the old structures of "doing what you're told" are out. No one can thrive in a

---

TREATING PEOPLE AS EQUALS IS FUNDAMENTAL TO CREATIVITY...

Just look at how younger generations flock to companies that do this. Students fresh from college call their CEOs by their first name, and they are connected to the biggest leaders in the field via social networks. There is no longer an "experience" over "talent" sentiment.

New employees grew up being more engaged with people, even chatting with politicians, celebrities, journalists, and commentators online. What they don't want is a suppressive environment where they cannot contribute and add their DNA to their work. There is a new work environment that is emerging with new expectations. Pay attention so you, as manager, can adapt as well.

---

creative environment when there is too much of a traditional hierarchy going on.

Companies like Google that reject this anti-hierarchy structure are benefitting enormously, as they are the ones attracting the world's greatest technical and business minds. If you need your company to do the same, then taking this concept in hand is something you have to do.

Once the people in your company understand how PEOPLE can suppress creativity, they can work towards correcting the issue. It will make for a better working environment for everyone—new and old.

Equality and Creative Control

They say that to nurture business creativity, a company needs to practice equality. I agree with this statement 100%.

Researchers from the University of Toronto discovered that the world's most successful economies were combined with high levels of creativity and innovation with low levels of inequality.

But equality in the workplace is so much more than implementing some progressive anti-discrimination policies or having a diverse hiring plan. Equality is not just about race, gender, or sexual orientation; it's about respect. And that's what matters! We already know that treating employees with respect is the reason why productivity increases.

What we're still learning is just how much respect impacts creative flow in a company. If you think about it, it makes perfect sense. I've always worked hard to make sure that my employees are happy, productive, and inspired—and a big part of this has been because I treat them as equals, as PEOPLE, and not interchangeable drones.

I've seen other managers in different companies mistreat their employees a heightened sense of themselves. These managers sometimes do not even recognize their behaviors because they have gotten away with it.

You have to consider these things in your workplace dynamic. Spreading creativity in your company and controlling it always comes at a price. You'll have to identify who in your company doesn't treat their employees as equals. Then you'll have to either train them or fire them. It is part of your new innovative commitment.

But because creativity is such a valued commodity—and it resides in your workforce—you can't have any negative influences removing all the creativity out of an area. You will have to make the hard decisions. You have to be extremely careful who you put in charge of people, as they greatly influence how that team will function and perform.

Stay close and occasionally speak to your employees about equality and how it can be improved in your working environment. Ask them to write down three things that describe the perfect boss. You'll be surprised what people will reveal about their present work environment. You need to be closer to potential issues that are affecting your human assets.

Collect suggestions from your employees and management for this, and see if it does anything to improve the creativity levels in the office. You'll often be able to see how much of an impact a little bit of respect has on a group of people.

CHAPTER 9

Challenges with Idea Collaboration

"If you have an apple and I have an apple and we exchange these apples then you and I will still each have one apple. But if you have an idea and I have an idea and we exchange these ideas, then each of us will have two ideas."

GEORGE BERNARD SHAW

The collaborative process for developing innovation requires a mix of internal and external resources and inputs, with forward-looking companies involving customers, partners, and third-party experts. The necessity of collaboration is pivotal in today's information technology sector by knowledge workers.

A 2012 report conducted by the McKinsey Global Institute suggested that knowledge workers spend 28 hours each week writing emails, searching for information, and collaborating internally. Interactive tools common in today's work environment could represent a 20–25 percent improvement in productivity. Access to social media also could reduce information searching time by as much as 35 percent—returning over 6 percent of an innovation worker's time. The access to real-time interactivity via video conferencing, instant messaging, and conference calling and the availability of real-time data make the collaboration effort much more effective than it has ever been.

Other findings of the McKinsey Global Institute study include:

- Just 3 percent of companies are "fully networked" and using social media to interact with customers, partners, and employees.
- In the U.S., only 5 percent of all communications and content takes place on social networks.
- Companies that seek consumer input to drive product development have an opportunity to generate consumer insights and market intelligence via social media.
- Social technologies could add an estimated $170–200 billion in value annually for advanced industries.

So, with all the access available to companies and knowledge workers, it is still not the normal practice, operationally or environmentally.

The Large Hadron Collider (LHC)[11] is the world's largest and highest-energy particle accelerator, located in a tunnel 17 miles (27 kilometers) in circumference beneath the Franco-Swiss border near Geneva, Switzerland. The European Organization for Nuclear Research (CERN) built it during 1998 to 2008, with the aim of allowing physicists to test the predictions of different theories of particle physics and high-

---

11   Large Hadron Collider. *Wikipedia, the free encyclopedia.* <https://mail.google. com/mail/?shva=1#inbox/13d17f04aace746b>

energy physics and particularly prove or disprove the existence of new particles theories.

The LHC was built in collaboration with over 10,000 scientists and engineers from over 100 countries, as well as hundreds of universities and laboratories.

Considering the number of collaborators and institutions involved, delays were relatively few, but sometimes took a year or more to resolve. A collaborative undertaking of this magnitude in size, vision, and reach is unparalleled to the projects most of us undertake in our business lives. However, complications that can occur are not dissimilar in any collaborative effort.

The Idea Lifecycle and Efficiency

Based on the principles of the idea lifecycle, issues are bound to arise when considering how effective processes like search and mixing will be. You will face these common challenges and overcome them for your team and company. Idea collaboration will sit at the core of nearly all of your projects, so this is not something to be taken lightly.

The idea lifecycle is a formal process for managing the lifecycle of ideas in an organization from generation and conversion to realization and exploitation in the marketplace. It is a key part of innovation management.

Ruling out Search, Mixing and Insight Methodologies

Older methodologies may no longer be relevant if they are not producing valid returns on the investment (time and money). There are methods that are still used today that must be reexamined as useful when applied. I offer these as a warning on potential outcomes:

1. *Search:* You can begin to see why some experts believe that the search intuition is inherently useless. People that want to

generate ideas can only do it if they are prepared to "wander the maze"—trying many different routes and methods until something is discovered. These searches can be fruitless, but it depends on the person doing the searching.

2. *Mixing:* Likewise the idea mixing structure is also simple but fairly ineffective, according to some experts. People will simply have to try and match their ideas until something fits. That means trying different combinations, discussing different viewpoints, brainstorming, and trying to make a few good ideas into one great idea.

3. *Insight:* The same goes for insight; it's unreliable and happens when it wants to.

So, essentially you may have been using three fairly unstable intuitive elements to create an idea lifecycle, even though it may not work at all. These accounts imply that, to increase creativity, all you have to do is encourage people to do more searches and more mixes.

This is the old school way of thinking, which is why creativity was never valued. Now, with the rise of technology and the increase in the overall value of creative talent, it's completely different. Yes, generating great ideas is hard, but that's part of the challenge.

As we begin to understand more about the creative process, we will come up with systematic ways to change how efficient people move through the entire creative idea-generation process. It's like Mr. Shaw says in the quote-ideas spread like wildfire. Even though they are fairly intangible and hard to nail down, they have a way of getting out.

This chapter is about learning more on the various challenges and opportunities you'll face when using the idea generation lifecycle in a business context. I will detail some strategies on how you can improve the efficiency of this system to boost the creative quality of your team.

ACCEPTABLE METHODOLOGY MANAGEMENT

Monitoring the progress of individuals is key to changing your idea generation processes from habitual to creative. Methodologies and tools play an important part in managing projects effectively among teams.

Methodology Defined:

A methodology is a set of methods, processes, and practices that are repeatedly carried out to deliver projects that may differ depending on the standards used among different industries. It describes every step in the project life-cycle in depth, so you know exactly which tasks to complete, when to do so, and how.

Methodology Benefits:

- Creates a project roadmap
- Monitors time, cost, and quality
- Controls change and scope (guard against "scope creep")
- Minimizes risks and issues
- Manages staff and vendors

Project Management Tool Considerations:

- It should provide a core set of processes to follow for delivering projects.
- Have a set of templates to help you build deliverables quickly.
- Provide a suite of case studies to help you learn from past projects.
- Make sure you have the ability to customize the methodology you will use.
- Provide the capability to import your existing processes into it.

Examples of Project Management Methods:

- **AdPM** – a best practices project methodology

- **MBP- Managing by Project from X-Pert Group,** Program and Project Management methodology and services

- **MSF - Microsoft Solutions Framework** is a set of principles, models, disciplines, concepts, and guidelines for delivering information technology solutions.

- **MITP – Managing Information Technology Projects,** IBM's established project management delivery method

- **MPMM - Project Management Methodology Manager or called 123 Project Management** is based on the worldwide project management standards PMBOK and Prince2 and contains all of the project management templates, forms, and checklists required.

- **PRINCE- Projects IN Controlled Environments** is a project management method. It covers the management, control, and organization of a project

- **Ten Step Project Management Process** is a methodology for managing work as a project, and it's designed to be as flexible as you need to manage your project

- **UPMM – Unified Project Management methodology** is based on suite of knowledge management tools

You will have to fit the methodology to your environment and industry standard. There are many more and even custom methods that are unique to a company. When you enter a new company or adapt a new method, pay attention to the efficiencies it offers and what can be improved upon. You never want to become mired in complacency and need to always question process as part of your innovative environment commitment.

There are four challenges that you will need to overcome in order to pave the way to problem identification. These models are:

1. The Core Conception Model
2. The Main Elaboration Model
3. The Key Accommodation Model
4. A-Z Challenges during the Full Cycle

1. The Core Conception Model

A simple way of understanding the problems that arise with conception is to understand how it works. It requires that people tend to their problems and identify information that is outside of their problem—for potential inclusion.

In other words, to come up with a solution, outside information needs to be considered. A common problem during this process is that "search inertia" occurs where the person doesn't feel like doing any more searching for potential solutions. They are resistant to change and instead choose to use the old school way of searching for answers.

These habitual, boring, absorbing, and predictable searches are not creative in any way, and they keep people in the problem-solving loop and out of the creativity loop. You can't do both; you can either choose one or the other. Habitual searching is something the business would have mocked up as a process that people should follow.

Another issue is that the concepts that people use to represent their goals, elements, and actions can distort or filter out information. This essentially hides or obscures the information your employees need to formulate a problem representation.

Even if your employees decide that they want to think differently, they won't be able to because their goals, elements, and actions are inconsistent with their initial problem representations. This can cause some adaptation issues.

Plus, search processes that they've learned at institutions or in other professions, organizations, or workgroups will influence your employees. Knowledge at these places is always shaped according to the institutions' beliefs and not what makes for a more creative line of search thinking.

Search inertia can keep people from considering any changes to a good idea, which will render that idea average. Instead of taking that risky step and searching in new ways to add different dimensions to your project, nothing is done. As a result, greatness is never achieved.

When search inertia is low, people find is easier to enter the creativity cycle, and ideas begin to burst from them. Low search inertia happens when research on problem finding, failure to create a problem representation, failing to find solutions, taking breaks, and reflecting on work done—are all times that your employees can capitalize on search inertia.

The moral here is that to overcome these challenges, you have to be open to trying new things and focusing on different areas—quite unlike anything you've done before. If the idea can survive the concept phase, then it's on to the main elaboration challenges.

2. The Main Elaboration Model

Elaboration is a crucial part of the creativity process, and it involves developing an incomplete initial insight into what is already a full understanding of the problem. Elaboration may be one of the most challenging features, as you can't guide people's examination of concepts and whether it is relevant, fits in, or goes well with different ideas.

Elaboration often happens within teams during meetings on a particular project. This can cause a whole new set of issues as different people's conceptions are challenged. Because of this, some highly creative people may never get to take advantage of the opportunity posed by conception before elaboration can be produced.

If the teams work well together, they should be able to elaborate on the proposed ideas and form an entirely new representation for you to work with. If this elaboration process happens, then it can be more valuable than "aha!" insight. You should see an entire team working seamlessly towards the goal of elaboration—it is an awesome view!

One slightly altered problem representation and it could change an entire new product line. Multiple reinterpretations must be found and examined so that the right decisions are made for the team and the company. Many of these problem representations are open to change, which can make the elaboration process unpredictable.

Problem-solving search is wonderfully dependable, but again—not part of the creative process. It's easier to problem-solve search, though elaboration is better for the project. This is one reason why elaboration is considered slacking; because very little is sometimes done during this phase of the project.

You'll also get organizational pressure to perform in your job, which can make switching from habitual search to creative search and elaboration so much harder. Experts have also predicted that elaboration is sensitive to moderating effects of socio-emotional factors, like psychological safety.

Reinterpretations of ideas may not be the final end result everyone is looking for, but they are the starting points that you need to take if new ideas, products, and search results are going to be used. There is no guarantee that one idea leads to a new product. It often takes many, many ideas—conceived and then reinterpreted.

Nicola Tesla had one big idea about energy, and this led to a lifetime's worth of work, experimentation, and problem solving. To make sense of it all—with this model—creativity can be more efficient when you use representations to generate ideas for end products and for problems that need to be reinterpreted.

The switch from old habitual forms of finding answers will be the biggest challenge, but I believe that with practice, guidance, and a creative attitude, your employees will take to this idea generation lifecycle. It's easy to conceive if you believe!

3. The Key Accommodation Model

"Many ideas grow better when transplanted into another mind than the one where they sprang up."
OLIVER WENDELL HOLMES

There are many things that can happen when a team of people changes the interpretation of a problem. It creates cognitive challenges for the project and representational gaps. These gaps mean that different people will understand the problem in the team differently and often in extremely incompatible ways.

This incompatibility is also a way to create opportunities, however. Elaboration may have caused clashes, but accommodation is the time to iron them out. Originators of the idea need to help others understand it and apply the correct cognitive mechanisms to interpret the knowledge accurately.

To properly speak activation, re-categorization, and juxtaposition to advance accommodation, these idea originators must draw on their team's knowledge. It's their goal to lead others to new ideas during this phase of accommodation. It will encourage everyone to get involved in the creativity lifecycle.

Problems may be nested, which will lead people to think about and accommodate the originators' reinterpretations of an idea. It can therefore be said that accommodation prompts others within your company to join in at the conception or elaboration phase—which will skip earlier challenges.

GIVING OTHER PEOPLE A CHANCE TO SHOW OFF THEIR CREATIVITY...

Is one of the best ways to accommodate a team dynamic. When you, as the creative control manager, go out of your way to understand their reinterpretations of the problem, the team will as well.

Any and all end-product ideas begin as little, not-so-important ideas. Then they go through the conception and elaboration process and become better. Use your team to crowd source this information for better outcomes.

NASH & PARETO EXPLAINED:

Nash equilibrium is a solution concept of a non-cooperative game involving two or more players, in which each player is assumed to know the equilibrium strategies of the other players, and no player has anything to gain by changing only his own strategy unilaterally. If each player has chosen a strategy and no player can benefit by changing strategies while the other players keep theirs unchanged, then the current set of strategy choices and the corresponding payoffs constitute a Nash equilibrium.

Stated simply, Brian and Tatiana are in Nash equilibrium if Tatiana is making the best decision she can, taking into account Brian's decision, and Brian is making the best decision he can, taking into account Tatiana's decision. Likewise, a group of players are in Nash equilibrium if each one is making the best decision that he or she can, taking into account the decisions of the others.

Pareto optimality is an outcome if there is no other outcome that makes every player at least as well off and at least one player strictly better off. A Pareto Optimal outcome cannot be improved upon without hurting at least one player. Often a Nash equilibrium is not Pareto optimal, implying that the players' payoffs can all be increased.

Accommodating other people's ideas is more than simply listening to what they have to say. It causes closeness in the team, mutual respect, and understanding—all of which improves the creativity of the group.

Nobel laureate Thomas Schelling said that game theory allowed anyone to characterize and analyze a large variety of situations whose outcomes depended on a choice of different people. Even though game theory itself doesn't offer any solutions to the dilemmas it raises, it's still a useful thing to know.

Game theory was once a productive change in representations used to evaluate strategic interactions. It also provided a basis for elaboration that resulted in very useful concepts like Nash equilibrium and Pareto optimality.

The contributions that this idea made alone validate its existence. And so it is with ideas that flow through the workplace. While there will always be clashes, problems, and inconsistencies at the accommodation stage, it's about shaping the idea into its final form by using the collective might of your team.

4. A–Z Challenges

This "concept–elaboration–accommodation model" implies that the creative process hinges on the successful completion of these phases. The challenge, of course, is to be consistent and to progress through the entire creative lifecycle rather than giving way to old habits or allowing problems to derail your focus.

To adequately support this model, you need to promote the effectiveness of all parts that make up the lifecycle and not just parts of it. The solution for side-stepping these challenges is to sustain an active interest in the problem and how to solve it. There are many factors that play a role in this.

You must be a master at goal setting, excellent at enabling intrinsic motivation in others, and have the ability to sustain prolonged concentration on the problem. That means you'll need high energy levels, persistence, and an iron will throughout the process.

"Intrinsic motivation" is the key concept here because it actively fosters persistence in tending to a problem representation. It also allows you to consider possible reinterpretations as you seek the answers to your problem.

You are driven to pursue any and all courses of action that may lead you to the correct answer. While intrinsic motivation doesn't trigger cognitive mechanisms, it is partially responsible for people making it through the fairly unpredictable creative lifecycle.

Intrinsic motivation can then be used as a mediating mechanism for mixed evidence to produce creative end products. This motivation will eventually be coupled with a factor that sets off the cognitive mechanisms in your mind, which will produce the reinterpretations that you need. It's a great basis for generating fresh ideas and excellent end products.

Multiple factors need to be combined to address the varying concerns in the creativity lifecycle. What is most important in this model is the breadth of support and coverage of these crucial phases. If you only facilitate elaboration and not accommodation, it will be less effective. If you only take conception into account and leave out elaboration, it will be less effective.

The general rule is this: "The more aspects of the creative lifecycle that a collection of factors facilitate, the more that collection should facilitate the production of new ideas." Many different factors can trigger creativity—like intrinsic motivation—and these should, in turn, trigger cognitive mechanisms for idea generation.

These issues that come built into the creative lifecycle suggest that creativity, in its purest form, is malleable. These processes aren't inefficient if the people that are using them know and understand the risks involved.

With creativity there will always be this "risk" of inefficiency, but if you focus on individual cognitive challenges and helping each team member and the team as a whole to work on these phases, there is no reason why this can't be an excellent way to improve the creative lifecycle in your company.

Problem Solving with Innovators

Creative people are always charged and ready to solve problems in new and exciting ways. That's why the largest tech companies in the world have developed processes that make it easy to implement these creative problem-solving systems.

When your team is handed a problem, they will need to get to work on figuring out how to solve this problem for people by creating a new, innovative product that will not only sell but sell well. It's a very difficult thing to do, if you don't have these steps to use:

- **Objective finding:** What are your objectives? I mean ALL of your objectives. It's important to lay them all out for your team to see so that they have all of the information and can use it in their cognitive processes.
- **Fact finding:** Once all of the data has been given to your team, release them into the wild for research purposes. Who is involved, what's involved, when, where, why, and how? Answering basic questions will lead your team down the right path. Once these are detailed, add feelings, lists, perceptions, and notes to the mix. Use all the data to formulate a search process that results in innovative answers.
- **Problem finding:** All ideas have problems and challenges. What are yours? What sort of opportunities do they represent? Focus on the right problem; the one that will rapidly improve your idea. Redefine what you

want, add things, take things away, and experiment with different ideas.

- **Idea finding:** Brainstorm and generate ideas. Take some time to come up with wild, outside-the-box ideas that will take your mind down new paths. Explore these ideas, and evaluate whether they can be solutions to your core problem. Take risks, try idea combinations, and find innovations in the mystery!

- **Solution finding:** Take your best ideas and improve them by making them stronger and clearer. Create the criteria needed to evaluate the ideas for success. Use these criteria to separate the top idea from the others. Which is most likely to solve the problem? Is it ready to be implemented?

- **Acceptance finding:** Propose your idea to your team. Look at who is responsible for it and who has to do what and by when. What sorts of resources are available to you? Then realize this idea by transforming it into a fully-fledged, active solution!

Getting Project Closure

Your company has made a considerable investment of money, resources, and time, and most of the people involved in a project are most likely ready to move on to other business. It is time to pass the torch of this project over to marketing, operations, or to new ownership so the team can begin to fix something else.

Before you close out a project and wipe your hands clean of it, there are a few issues to review:

1. **Project Evaluation:** How did the project finalize in budget, risks, and other considerations? What additional steps are needed to close the administration and idea

lifecycle before it is passed to the next parties? Teams will need to consider the detail of their creation for it to be a realized effort. If not, it will cost the company additional time, money, and resources to recalibrate the effort.

2. **Project Outcome Assessment:** Before you pass this over the fence to another department, make sure all the necessary sign-off was accepted that warrants market viability. There may be a need for more project management if adequate acceptances were not met. Do not be too eager to move the product, project, or idea to the next level if you do not have 100% acceptance.

3. **Find Templates in the Experience:** Records should be made of the project and process so it can be added to learn and build new efficiencies. There must be gems discovered that can be retooled and used again in another project so innovation moves even faster next time.

4. **Schedule a Party!** With all the necessary reviews, sign-off, and successful completion of this effort, do not forget to get the entire company involved in the birth of this new project, product, or idea. Everyone deserves to be recognized and celebrated. You need to show your commitment to these highly creative assets you have created and celebrate your highly innovative and exciting enterprise. Besides, it's a great reason to party!

CHAPTER 10

CREATE — The Key to Perfect Innovation

"The creative process is also the most terrifying part because you don't know exactly what's going to happen or where it is going to lead. You don't know what new dangers and challenges you'll find."

STEPHEN COVEY

The creation of something new feels personal and can be the most rewarding and satisfying event you can experience. Giving life, in any form, is full of wonderful rewards. The drive of emotions at the beginning, middle, and end are reasons we, as humans, need to create, innovate, and repeat this amazing gift that is in every one of us. It does not matter what we create as long as we (you) are creating.

Instead of the usual, "How was your day?" I am known to ask my family a different type of question. "What did you create today?" This is a great way to begin a conversation and allows each of us to think about our contribution to our world around us. This gives us, young and old family members, a chance to reflect each day on how we have impacted those around us in a positive way. It also suggests that we have ownership in our lives. If we are not creating, what are we doing?

I believe we all achieve our highest level of fulfillment and are happiest when we are creating. It is our human right to create. No one can prevent us from using our imagination to create and contribute to the process. The science fiction author Ray Bradbury once said, *"The ability to fantasize is the ability to survive."*

The word CREATE is the most important word in any language because it connotes the expression of giving—the food for the soul, life in the making, and interaction with our environment that connects us. These attributes are innate in the activity of creating. While the process always takes work and initiative, the end reward is satisfaction, a higher sense of self, and symbiotic relationship to others.

The pure definition of the word "create" is always positively charged. Synonyms such as Make, Produce, Build, Conceive, Compose, Appoint, Imagine, Plan, Shape, Start, and Establish are a few of the highly productive descriptions. I cannot think of another word that sets the imagination on fire like this word, this activity.

Imagine that each day began with the thought of this single word—CREATE. What will I create today? What will I Conceive, Build, Shape, Plan, Invent to make my world and the world around me better? I am wondering what others at work will CREATE.

How exciting your company will become with this single word! CREATE!

Everything that we have discussed so far has led you to this point. This is the ultimate *key* that unlocks the secret to your perfect innovations, your perfect company, and your perfect life. You now know that once you have fully integrated the creative gene company wide, you will have the fulfillment that you wish for your company.

Remember, you are trying to achieve:

- Improved employee contribution at all levels of your company
- A company that has an organic reputation for quality
- An environment where all feel ownership in every aspect of your business
- The desire and drive to achieve excellence within all of your people
- The ability to accomplish the market differentiation for your business
- Complete control of the company's Creative Control environment

It all starts with this rather simplistic understanding of the will and need to CREATE. You now have all the right reasons to position your company and its employees for 100% capacity of their attention, output, and desires to be their best.

To further solidify your action steps to unleash your ability to transform, improve, and heighten your company's creative and innovative output, I will teach you the six steps to perfect innovation.

The CREATE System is a highly effective program that I have taught and used in my own career. Not only does it lift the innovative environment while strengthening the collaborative contribution, it also perpetuates ownership at all levels of your company and invites new talent to you, organically.

1. Conceptualize
2. Relate
3. Embody
4. Actualize
5. Triumph
6. Evangelize

Each of these concepts will give you all the details you will need to communicate the new CREATE process that you will be using in your company daily.

1. Conceptualization

The first stage involves Conceptualization. This is the foundation to exercising, expanding, and developing the scope of your intention. When conceptualizing a new idea, it is essential to direct the thinking to the framework questions and gather answers to help evolve the idea through the various stages of its lifecycle. Bill Gates did not invent Windows, but conceptualized the process by which users would interact with the operating system.

Impacts on developing your solutions include your environment and market overlapped with the strategic vision of your company. If our corporate objective is to deliver movies on every device, you must align with broad opportunities that will fulfill that objective. If your strategic vision is to change the way people make phone calls, your innovation process has to align with solving new, potentially disruptive ideas that will accomplish the mission. The business model is the framework for the conceptualization process. With that, your teams will consider the customer need, market environment, competition, business strategy of the enterprise, and the ecosystem consisting of partners and suppliers in the market for the design of the idea.

Good conceptualizers will have a laser-focus understanding for the strategic vision and the business model it supports. The collaboration effort will play effective when everyone is of equal understanding for the vision and how that vision will be marketable (e.g., make money).

There are four phases of the conceptualization framework. They are:

Phase I.   Concise understanding for the strategic vision
Phase II.   Business model alignment
Phase III. Differentiation (ours and theirs)
Phase IV.   Complexity (costs and time)

The Strategic Vision of the company is your roadmap, and without complete understanding of that vision by your creative and innovation teams, you will not achieve your mission-critical goals. Yes, some things do happen by accident, but without a guided and concerted effort, the project can get lost at the onset of the conceptualization stage. The vision keeps us grounded on outcomes and objectives.

The business model alignment suggests that we all currently understand how we make money and how any new idea or innovation will connect to the current business model. What will be the distribution, profit and costs, and overall benefit structure? Remember when Netflix reconsidered their consumer model after going out strong on its new model?

When we are conceptualizing what new ideas we can bring to the company, we need to understand the relationship between our current product mix and our competitors' product offerings. Samsung is constantly looking at the direction and consumer acceptance of Apple products.

How complex the new idea is in regards to time and money will also have an effect on your initial planning process. Sometimes the ground rules may be to provide ideas without limitations, but in most situations, your product or idea generations will involve a focused vision with expectations on when it can get to the market.

It is the interpretation of a problem, objective, or phenomenon that forms our concepts. Our intent is solely to conceive the ideas that will adhere to the strategic vision while determining the most efficient means to differentiate us from the competition. Our ability to conceptualize every problem solving, revolutionary, or potentially disruptive innovation lies in our and our team's ability to reason and then relate.

2. Relate

The second stage of the CREATE process is to **R**elate your idea to something else. That means establishing logical or causal connections between your idea and the rest of your team's ideas. We begin to form our relationship with our ideas and the rest of the world. It becomes an internal-external or inside-out relationship that must become symbiotic in a natural and organic way.

The relationship between your creativity and your innovations is symbiotic as they are complementary partners, natural and organic. When you can see the interconnectedness between new ideas for products and their connection to different things, such as how these new products will interact with the market, you start to expand your ability to create in a related and interoperable manner. If we create a new digital music format and there are no devices that can deliver our new format, our ability to meet the customers' needs are not met. Conversely, if I am able to create a new digital music format that costs less to use, is easier to adapt to other digital devices, and may allow for new high-speed video compression, now I am operating in a *related manner* that is considering all aspects of my business environment.

Sometimes two good ideas can be combined to create something incredible—or two unusual ideas are combined that leads to a breakthrough in the creative process. It's your job to listen to all of the proposed ideas and then see which ones relate the best to each other. These can be evident, but sometimes they're not evident at all.

For example, sometimes a vintage design idea can be combined with an airplane design theme to result in something special. The designers will take these two concepts, combine them, and come up with something new and exciting for the market.

There is a new sandwich on the market that is selling like crazy—rocket salad and curry. Chances are this was not around a few years ago, as it's totally new. People absolutely love it because it's a little strange. If you can combine two ideas and make something unusual or unique, that's even better.

In a way, the product has a piece of everyone in it and is therefore far more likely to appeal to a broader audience. This is especially true in app creation. Creating weird games sounds easy, but it's devastatingly hard. Plants vs. Zombies was a great example of a super-weird game that went viral and ended up making the creators millions of dollars.

So take this time to finalize your concept. See what the absurd combinations look like and how they function. Try to answer the original question with a solution so powerful that no one in the world will be able to resist buying your incredible product.

3. Embody

The third stage of the CREATE process is to make sure that your ideas Embody your proposed vision, goals, elements, and actions. To embody something means to make it "concrete" or perceptible to others. If you're going to do that with your shiny new idea, you will need your entire team onboard.

You've probably heard the statement, "You are what you eat." Well, with product innovation, your outcomes are the reflection of your company. Whether we are improving the effectiveness or efficiency of our coding team by reducing the error rates or simply improving the quality rates on improved time, we are trying to create a new embodiment of our methods, thus improving our organization.

Product and process improvements are overlapping and simultaneous activities when it comes to developing new ideas and innovation. There is a cause and effect that must be considered on each step. Some integration may go without process overhaul, and others may require a complete new set of process standards. These, in fact, may kill the idea or become the catalyst for identifying a new procedural method.

In business, the S-Curve performance is a type of curve that shows the growth of a variable in terms of another variable, often expressed as units of time.

For example, an S-Curve of the growth of company sales for a new product would show a rapid, exponential increase in sales for a period of time, followed by a tapering or leveling off. The tapering occurs when the population of new customers declines. At this point, growth is slow or negligible and is sustained by existing customers that continue to buy the product. This is when your team has the correct data and performance tools that allow them to problem solve, introduce new products, and become the embodiment of the mission.

Remember, you now have a full team of creators and idea generators. It's time to unleash their talents, to see how they embody the creative process as they transform ideas from something intangible into something marketable.

Within the embodiment stage, having the right tools and resources available is critical so that your company truly embodies that of an innovative enterprise. If you are investing in an environmental shift that totally respects and values your creative enterprise, the tools that allow for efficiencies and effective operations must be available and used as part of a fully appreciated product cycle. Access to data, shared enterprise technologies, and project management methods alignment must be considered so your teams can directly impact changes to performance in the market, like issues affecting the S-Curve of performance.

Creating a prototype or working on the programming for something brand new is a very exciting process. The key is to not lose anything in translation, which is where embodying your idea comes in. You'll have notes and research about it, but now you need to work with your team on creating one solid idea scope that details the project from head to toe. This keeps everyone grounded and on the mission of the project. Once everyone is happy with the level of detail and refinement in the concrete scope, you can move on to the next stage of the creation process.

A large part of working through the embodiment stage is defining the problems and ironing them out. That's why creating a detailed work scope is so essential. So many companies come up with great ideas, and then the core of them gets lost when they are handed over to the people that bring the idea to life. It is critical that, if this is the case in your company, you retool this process immediately so ownership is embodied.

4. Actualize

The fourth stage in the CREATE process is to **A**ctualize your idea by physically creating it, by making it real! There are few things as pleasurable to a team of people than seeing a great idea come to life. Execution of an idea can make or break your entire process.

What builds the desire to execute and complete a project lies in motivation. Unleashing this motivational force is what every one of your team members bring to work, to their ideas, and ultimately to the fulfillment stages. This is a powerful force because once an employee has tapped into the values that improve their motivation, anything, I mean anything, is possible. Some people call it personal drive, but regardless, understanding the mechanisms that propel the individual to excel is there in all of us.

You may recall the example I used earlier about asking a skier what they like best about skiing. Their response was the exhilaration they feel when they get a chance to ski fresh powder. I ask them to tap into that emotion, then asked them to take on a project. If we can get our staff to understand the excitement emotion that drives us to seek excitement on off-time applied at work or tapped into at any time, any place, all tasks, obstacles, or challenges are an opportunity to gain fulfillment (perhaps an adrenaline rush).

These images of taking on a new task and seeing it to completion are wonderful gems that we as managers or creators have an opportunity to share and build upon.

Maslow's Hierarchy of Needs is a tried and true outline of our motivational levels, based on low basic needs to full actualized quests.

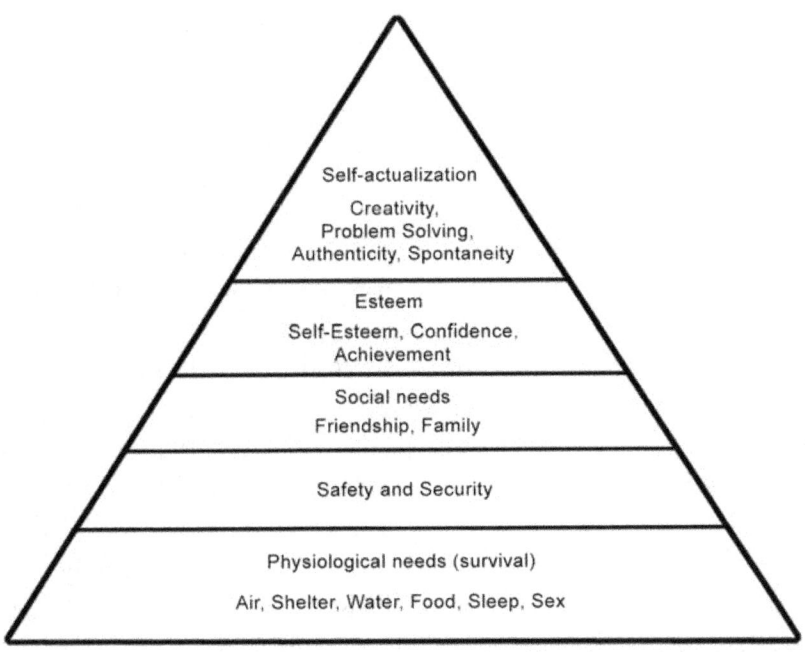

Figure 1: Maslow's Hierarchy of Needs

Maslow's Hierarchy of Needs[12] is based on the premise that every person is capable and has the desire to move up the hierarchy toward a level of self-actualization. The model includes:

1. *Physiological & Biological needs* – air, food, drink, shelter, warmth, sex, sleep, etc.
2. *Safety needs* – protection from elements, security, order, law, limits, stability, etc.
3. *Social needs* – work group, family, affection, relationships, etc.

---

12 Cherry, Kendra. Hierarchy of Needs. **About.com Guide.**
http://psychology.about.com/od/theoriesofpersonality/a/hierarchyneeds.htm

4. *Esteem needs* – self-esteem, achievement, mastery, independence, status, dominance, prestige, managerial responsibility, etc.
5. *Self-Actualization needs* – realizing personal potential, self-fulfillment, seeking personal growth, and peak experiences

These needs in life are the exact ones we face and try to achieve every day of our lives at work. If we are deficient of any of these, they may affect our performance and action. Just getting started can become a struggle. Once the individual develops enough trust in his or her safety, then they can focus on relationship needs. Here the individual seeks to establish connection and a sense of belongingness. This not only includes being loved but being able to give love as well. When an individual's love and relationship needs are mostly met, esteem needs come into play. This refers to the individual's need to have confidence in his or her self-worth. After an individual has mostly satisfied the basic needs, that person's attention shifts to the higher need for self-actualization.

Abraham Maslow described self-actualization needs this way:

> *"What a man can be, he must be. This need we may call self-actualization...It refers to the desire for self-fulfillment, namely, to the tendency for him to become actualized in what he is potentially. This tendency might be phrased as the desire to become more and more what one is, to become everything that one is capable of becoming."*

Overall, the same definition applies in today's world. Make people feel equal to embrace their contribution, give them the tools to push themselves, and show them that they can reach even further as their potential is unlimited.

Once the desire is there to actualize one's performance, the affects or influences (negative or positive) remain intact. The staff member can only envision their need to fulfill their best output. New drive, new performance, and new expectations are all outcomes to your creative commitment.

Now we are ready to have you and your team's ideas exist in the real world. Ideally, you want your idea to be highly successful in the real world. But that is going to take a specific process of creation. At this point, you have all of the details you need to move forward with actualized precision.

Standard operating procedures like scope plans to keep everyone on track, feasibility studies, competitive analysis, and project management processes and methodologies all become less important, as they serve only to strengthen the ideas. Those innovations become the differentiators that have been fully actualized by a group of highly motivated and high performance individuals.

Your ideas will become more and more powerful if you use the processes found in this book. Step by step, inch-by-inch—you'll be able to actualize some of the greatest people and innovations your company has ever produced.

5. Triumph

The fifth stage in the CREATE process is to Triumph over adversity and your competitors by continually developing your creative control environment. The process by which you and your teams have overcome all the challenges, expected and unexpected, are amazing accomplishments. We should not be shy, and it is not time to be humble in expressing our excitement about starting, identifying, or completing a project. Whether the new innovation is new to you or to your industry or competitors, it needs to be recognized as an event.

Let's imagine for a moment that you and your company just created an event that was like the very popular Angry Birds game. You imagine it is going to be a normal launch with your expectations in check. You cannot even visualize that at some point this little slingshot game is going to become the example that every other software company is going to try to achieve. The Birds are now on tee shirts, board games sold in big box stores, and part of our social conscience. Are you finished, or do you tap into the reinvention, repackaging, and version update like crazy new features? You consider raising the price, engage more brand licensing agreements, and think about a full-featured movie. Is that it?

Of course that is not it! You are going to replicate, exploit the opportunity, and continue to lead your industry. You are now king of your hill! Winners! Victors! Innovators! This is a triumph for management, staff, developers, project managers, accountants, staff attorneys, and even the mail carrier that delivers your mail. They all feel that sense of pride in knowing your company and feel ownership as a result of their contribution.

Recently, Kraft Foods, the $18 billion dollar in revenues food products company, with iconic brands like Maxwell House, Oscar Mayer, and JELL-O, announced a new commitment to "innovate and contemporize" its product offerings. After three years of development, they tried to get their "groove back" by moving away from their "field of dreams" strategy of "if we launch it, they will come."

In 2010 Kraft[13] decided to focus on the big ideas. The act of focusing contributed to the birth of three new $100 million platforms: MiO beverage mixes, Oscar Mayer Selects deli meats, and Velveeta Skillet packaged meals.

---

13   Kraft Celebrates Product Innovation 'Heroes & Rock Stars.' *CSPnet.com* http://www.cspnet.com/news/general-merchandise/articles/kraft-celebrates-product-innovation-heroes-rock-stars

They celebrated the innovators, making them the heroes and rock stars of the company. "Positive discontent" became the new mantra, encouraging employees to get angry and motivated enough to make change rather than disengaging.

Barry Calpino, vice president of breakthrough innovation, was quoted as saying, *"Year two is just as important and often more important than year one, but most companies pull way back after the launch year. We went just as big in year two as in year one."*

As a result of their commitment to innovation, they experienced strong new product growth: MiO grew more than 60% in that second year.

This effort showed Kraft's commitment and demonstrated to its employees that they were dedicated to new innovation and meant what they said, which further fueled the culture shift. Going forward, the company is committed to continuously learning and being consistent in execution.

Accomplishments are all laced with adversity. Internal to external environmental factors are prevalent everywhere and will come at the least optimal time. We have all experienced the printer breaking right before a board meeting or server going down before a demo presentation. How you have led your team to this point and training them on overcoming the adversity with grace and pride is an important part of the triumph stage.

It is part of your creative commitment to acknowledge and celebrate all accomplishments that lead to product innovation. You are committed to your team as they are the catalyst for accomplishments. Show them the "love" and appreciation, and it will come back to you ten-fold. As we learned from Maslow's Hierarchy of Needs, all people require some form of recognition. It is important to plan accordingly for the occasion and create an event for different stages of the cycles as they are all accomplishments.

Once you've gone the extra mile to make your team feel like winners, their creative confidence will build and good things will begin to happen. Triumph over the market by investing in your people and in the long-term success of your product as a key investment. The CREATE process will become your KEY for developing and accomplishing your strategic vision companywide.

6. Evangelize

The final part of the CREATE process is to Evangelize new initiatives, products, innovation, and your overall company. This means to completely embody your commitment to your innovation strategy by promoting, living, and celebrating every activity within your company.

It is not just you, your employees, or their family members that evangelize the amazing accomplishments of your company, but it is your end customers that are the strongest evangelists that money cannot buy. When customers are truly thrilled about their experience with your product or service, they can become outspoken evangelists for your company. This group of satisfied believers can be converted into a potent marketing force to grow your universe of customers, goodwill, and more business.

Customer evangelism is a way of capitalizing on the success of your products that are successfully used by their core customer base. They begin to serve as ambassadors of your brand and its product line. We all know that personal endorsements are far better than advertisement for learning about a new product or service. Using your team and customers to evangelize their experiences builds amazing marketing reach and saves your company millions. The use and efficacy of customer evangelism for a product or service to encourage other people to buy your products is the highest compliment.

Your products that are brought to light by personal endorsements is marketing at its optimal level. Their passion for the products is a requirement. Their positive experience with your products gives you an upper hand over your competitors.

These are the factors you need to engage internally and external as part of your Evangelism Stage:

1. Teamwork and Synergy Company-wide
2. Passion and Enthusiasm for Your Products and Capabilities
3. Full Awareness of Your Core Mission

Company & Product Evangelism makes it possible for total corporate objectives to be met since it forms a basis for all other objectives to be met. Your company is now on its way for full actuality of its strategic mission.

This will give you and your entire company the ability to apply the **CREATE Process** at any time, start again, and reload when needed. Either overall strategy or with new concepts, ideas, and new flagship products, CREATE is your tool for total innovation and creative control. As a process, this was designed to be a never-ending circle of improvement—gradually increasing your creative potential until your company is creating the best products in their class, in the world.

Create System 360 View

The CREATE System of: **C**onceptualize, **R**elate, **E**mbody, **A**ctualize, **T**riumph, and **E**vangelize is a powerful and active business system. Now that you have been given the key to operate in a fully functional and optimized innovative environment, you must keep yourself in the evaluation process. This, I assure you, will be that new car that never gets old and always retains that new car smell!

You must continue to ask yourself these key questions, and if any one of them is out of balance, you must recalibrate.

Have you:

- Improved employee contribution at all levels of your company?
- Created a company that has an organic reputation for quality?
- Developed an environment where all feel ownership?
- Identified the desire and drive to achieve excellence within all staff?
- Accomplish the market differentiation for your business?
- Positioned yourself to control the company's creative control environment?

The structure of this work is all based on creativity and your commitment to innovation. Everything from idea generation, product creation, and successful market launch to full employee appreciation are all that is needed to take your company to its next evolution. It's all part of your new innovation strategy.

These steps can be adapted to meet your needs, but keep the core concepts intact. Involve this process with your core team to begin immediately. And as always, never stop inspiring your company to be the most creative version of itself.

CHAPTER 11

The Idea Gene

"First comes thought; then organization of that thought, into ideas and plans; then transformation of those plans into reality. The beginning, as you will observe, is in your imagination."

NAPOLEON HILL

Do you know what an idea is worth? Different ideas have different values. Sometimes exceptional ideas never get developed, and no money is made. Sometimes bad ideas are developed, and a small fortune is made. What is going on here?

So how do you calculate the value of an idea? How do you turn ideas into money when you have no assurances that this will happen? The honest answer is that you don't. There are never any guarantees with the development of an idea. Innovative officers have to go on their business acumen, wisdom, instinct, and team effort to increase the odds of success. Every idea will not turn into gold, but carefully planned and executed ideas turn into innovation and innovation turns into new revenue.

"The only thing in life you can control: your own effort."
– MARK CUBAN

Mark Cuban, the billionaire owner of the Dallas Mavericks, explains that the one thing that he can control in his life is his effort. The same applies to business. The only thing any entrepreneur, salesperson, or anyone in any position can control is his or her effort.

In his book, *How to Win at Sports Business*, Cuban states that *"I had to kick myself in the ass and recommit to getting up early, staying up late, and consuming everything I possibly could to get an edge. I had to commit to making the effort to be as productive as I possibly could. It meant making sure that every hour of the day that I could contact a customer was selling time, and when customers were sleeping, I was doing things that prepared me to make more sales and to make my company better."*

He stated further that he had to make sure that he was not lying to himself about how hard he was working every day and not using hours in a day to measure his effort. Cuban believes that setting goals and getting results is the best measurement for effort. Things such as closing deals, overtaking a business segment, becoming the expert in his field, and keeping his edge have to be constantly considered.

Cuban also points out that it's not about working longer but working better by always setting goals and pushing for real results.

Effort certainly is a measurement if it results in great business deals and inspiring new innovation. Consumer acceptance for your products and measureable revenue growth are clear ways to assume your effort, creativity, and ingenuity are all working according to plan. But how should you think about your investment in creating a new, energized, innovative enterprise? What investments are best to give you optimal returns? When should you expand or contract operational activities?

How to Monetize Creativity

This brings us to another interesting perspective —you monetize your creative output by the people you hire, train, and nurture. Nurture is a word rarely used in today's fast-paced, high expectations, and sometimes under-appreciated business world. Surely there is some way to harness the power of creativity so that you can make money from it? Some ideas are worth millions, some billions. Then there are ideas that bomb and never earn a dime. But does this make it okay to treat ideas as some intangible concept instead of a real commodity?

Imagine for a moment that someone in your team has the potential to be the next Steve Jobs. Imagine if that person in your team, working for your company, came up with the next evolution of the X product, akin to the iPhone or iPad. It's a scary thing to consider that this person has provided your company with an idea that could sustain you for the next 10 years.

Now, here's another, more difficult question. If Bill Gates or Steve Jobs were in fact sitting in on one of your routine meetings, would their strange ideas be acknowledged or even accepted? I bet you're wondering about that and what it would look like.

"Hey, I have an idea! What if we create a small flat screen TV that fits in your hand and gives people the ability to watch movies, or access to millions of movies, books, songs, and video chat with their friends or co-workers, access the Internet, take pictures and record videos and send them to anyone instantaneously?"

How would this idea fly at your company? Too big? Not the

right people to execute it? You are not sure how to package it and get the funding? It is at these times that you must pause and see if this should be considered; how you could answer all the "what if" questions.

How many people in your team right now have excellent ideas but they don't speak up, or perhaps you're not keenly focused on that possibility?

If one idea from that Steve Jobs-like person made millions for your company, what would it be worth to you and to the other people that sat in on those meetings? These are all questions that center on money. Businesses pay people to work for them, but paying them for million dollar ideas is a convention that has not been established yet.

What has been established is that creative people are in demand. Their ideas are in demand. And there are steps that you can take to ensure that no other companies poach your best thinkers. At the end of the day, ideas are great, but it's the company that brings those ideas to life that really deserves the credit.

This is how companies make their money from creativity. They attract the finest creative talent, farm the best ideas from these people, and then put their significant resources to work bringing these great ideas into the real world.

On November 6, 2012, a patent (Patent No.: US D670,286 S) was granted to 15 inventors that was assigned to Apple Inc. of Cupertino, California, for rectangular devices with rounded corners that looked like this:

It was for the Portable Display

Device,[14] and yes, Steve Jobs was listed as one of the 15 inventors of this device. Questions are now emerging on the value and validity of patents, such as this device, and patents' effective use in limiting business and innovation advances.[15]

Michele Boldrin and David Levine of the research division of the Federal Reserve Bank of St. Louis argue there are strong economic grounds to abolish patents because "there is no empirical evidence that they serve to increase innovation and productivity, unless the latter is identified with the number of patents awarded—which, as evidence shows, has no correlation with measured productivity."

In fact, they argue, there may be good reason to believe they actively discourage productivity and innovation. And there's also the matter of how they are defined and enforced.

A notable observation being:

Patent litigation typically involves dying firms, which tend to accumulate stockpiles of patents but are no longer able to produce marketable products, suing new and innovative firms. Microsoft has become the chief among the patent trolls.

Personally, I have been raised in a business environment with the understanding that holding a patent is a good thing. Investors like them as it further protects their interests. It brings value and creates a competitive barrier. What's not to like about patents?

I have also learned that some companies use patents as their sole business model. They are unable to market and produce their intellectual ideas in the real world, so they wait for capable entrepreneurs to get market success and sue for "damages."

---

14   United States Design Patent. Patent No: US670286S
<http://assets.sbnation.com/assets/1701443/USD670286S1.pdf>

15   Boldrin, Michele & Levine, David K. The Case Against Patents. Research Division Federal Reserve Bank of St. Louis: Working Paper Series. http://research.stlouisfed.org/wp/2012/2012-035.pdf

There is a spider lurking, and the value of intellectual property can sometimes lie less on the workbench and more on the legal-bench.

The overall measurement of the creative output, from a monetary perspective, must be covered in due diligence procedure. This sometimes is a painful experience but so critical to realizing the full potential of your intellectual resources.

Finding Your Idea Moneymaker

It's going to take a while before you find that one single idea that lives up to its own potential. But in the meantime, great ideas are generated at your company every day. These ideas, while not perfect or executed perfectly, have a huge potential or you would not be working on them. Often ideas start out great, but they do not turn out as planned, or they do not pass feasibility or market trial tests. Finding your perfect new product will come given that you now know the CREATE System that will surely lead you to new innovation. Yes, it is at the core of your job, and your board, investors, and employees all count on your motivating factors that push your innovation team for urgency and solution-based processes.

You should understand that your next million-dollar idea does not happen overnight. It will be a process—a collection or mixture of smaller ideas integrated into each other over time. You might experience this early on in your creative control process. That's when you will really get inspired for using the creative control process.

Three things need to be considered daily to grow your business:

1. Should we improve a current product?
2. Shall we create a completely new product?
3. Do we acquire an underserved product?

Grow, Change, or Die – Negative Entropy and Equifinality

The theory of "negative entropy"[16] suggests that if you are not growing and changing, you are dying. It considers that to offset the natural degradation of a product or company, one must set up a structure where things are made, developed, and repaired to avoid closure. A good example of an organization that has experienced negative entropy would undoubtedly be the fast food chain giant McDonalds, which has managed to almost invade every country worldwide. By using external "energy," such as marketing and advertising, it has managed to survive when others have not.

Equifinality is a concept that states that a certain outcome can be achieved by many different means. For example, if a person decided she wished to take a stroll with her dog around their block, she would be faced with the choice of walking clockwise or counter-clockwise around it. Either will lead to the same desired outcome. In a business sense, it would be best to discover all the possible ways to achieve the set goals, then distinguish the best by considering all the factors involved with each possibility, and then choose the most efficient.

The introduction of the create control principles into your enterprise will do both: set up a systemic process by which your company will not slip into the abyss and put into play an effective product and processes.

Teams that are eager, like the individuals who support them, will take on every and any project thrown at them in the right framework. The contributions by all members will have a perpetuating effect on outcomes because they are aware, in the zone, and able to become your Steve Jobs. There is something

---

16   Evolution of organisational theory. <http://www.uplink.com.au/lawlibrary/Documents/Docs/Doc2.html>

extremely poetic once it all begins to work seamlessly.

The moral of the story is that your idea moneymaker is always just around the corner. The best thing you can do is implement a sound creative process, look after your employees, and take special precautions to go through the product development stages properly. Then, as you have positioned the advantages in your favor, the next big and many small things will start to happen. I guarantee it!

Optimizing Human Resources

Human resources departments are not always considered when companies are talking about ROI or the monetization of assets. But according the *Society for Human Resource Management*, the best HR practices always involve HR as part of the strategic planning effort. If all successful companies and entrepreneurs claim it is the people they hired who led them to profit, then we can easily assume that the people in your company are the most valuable assets you can have. With this new movement of hiring for increased innovative potential, businesses are searching for the right individuals to help them come up with better ideas. Get HR involved early and often.

To get optimal gain out of your workforce, you will have to implement a hiring process that invites creative people to your company; you need to be "followed" on LinkedIn and "liked" on Facebook to keep those potential assets close to you.

How do you make sure that your HR department is hiring the right people?

- Train your HR staff on the creative control principles and make sure they understand the CREATE ideologies of **C**onceptualize, **R**elate, **E**mbody, **A**ctualize, **T**riumph, and **E**vangelize.

- Do not rely purely on the online hiring platforms that segment based on certain keyword criteria. Be open-minded and reach a little deeper than just the top schools or Fortune 100 companies. Sometimes sifting through resumes and handling your own interviews pays off.
- Make sure that the job description that you put out into the world, along with the job posting, clearly articulates your company as an innovative and dynamic place to work. Insist that you have a creative business culture and that it is your driving force.
- When you finally get down to the candidate search and have to host interviews, speak to your applicants about their own creative processes and how they perceive innovation in the workplace.
- Shortlist the candidates that stand out, and invite them back for another interview before you decide. Have them attend an innovation planning session or participate in a product development exercise.
- Always look for creative candidates that work well with people, have a positive attitude, and have the potential to be advanced thinkers that will push others higher. These natural leaders will help spread your creative control ideology. Never employ below the peer group.

How to Spot Innovative Thinking

Innovative thinking is one of those things that come naturally to some people. Most of the resumes that land on your desk will be from traditional thinkers, those living in a comfort zone of organizational process and safe procedures. They have learned how to analyze the corporate temperament and push their good ideas only until it becomes politically detrimental.

The question is, how do you sort the innovative thinkers from the traditional thinkers? Innovative thinkers are obviously the better hire choice for an innovative enterprise. Everyone has different levels of innovation aptitude, no matter where they have worked previously. You can tell how valuable a person may be by discussing these questions.

20 Innovations Aptitude Assessment Questions

1. How do you define innovation and creativity?
2. What different types of innovative projects have you been involved with?
3. How do you spot opportunities for innovation?
4. How do you come up with an idea?
5. What is disruptive innovation?
6. What is the best way to disrupt a market?
7. What does "good enough" mean to you?
8. How do you know if your idea is good?
9. How do you get other people behind your idea?
10. How long does it take new products to scale?
11. Why do you think innovation is so important to our company?
12. Who are your innovation influences?
13. How would you encourage innovation in this organization?
14. How would you form and manage innovation teams?
15. What is in a good innovation strategy that you have been involved with?
16. What is the best way to manage an innovation portfolio?
17. What role should senior executives play in innovation?
18. How would you encourage others to become better innovators?

19. How would you quickly turn a good idea into a good business?

20. When do you know a new innovation is a bad idea?

Based on how they answer these questions, you will know whether they have a good innovative aptitude based on your commitment to the CREATE principles.

Retaining Your Creative Talent

How do you retain a creative talent that turns out to be invaluable to your business? If you are working in the tech hubs of Boston and Cambridge, Massachusetts, Silicon Alley of NYC, Silicon Valley area near San Francisco Bay, or Bangalore, India, Silicon Wadi of Tel Aviv, Israel, Silicon Gulf of the Philippines, and innovation hub locations in France, Germany, Spain, and the M4 Corridor between London and Reading, England, you know how important it is to attract and retain top talent. Top creative talent is always being snapped up by other companies, head hunters, and recruitment specialists. Just as quickly as they come, they could go.

The tech industry seems to be vast and limitless, but it's really like a group of gossiping teenagers. Everyone knows everyone else's business. If there is a creative talent in one of your teams who has done something really impressive, you need to put measures in place to keep that person satisfied or soon he or she will be off to greener pastures.

Here is how I've managed to retain some of my best employees using the CREATE principles.

Methods for stimulating top talent are:

1. Keep the innovation quotient high.
2. Keep the performance criteria interesting.
3. Push top performers to new challenges.

4. Keep rewards and recognition personal.
5. Involve top talent in leadership early.
6. Challenge and evaluate.
7. Promote the culture.

- **Keeping the innovation quotient high** is the process of making sure your top performers are constantly excited about the future. They need to be involved and challenged. You have to concern yourself with the elite performers as much as you need to cultivate the under-utilized. Their desire to achieve is not dissimilar. They need to be intellectually challenged with exciting and changing projects.
- **Performance criteria** are the measurements for raising the bar of output. Quality is far more important than quantity, but the expectation lies in the elite, and they wish to be thought of as high performers. Unless you continue to set new achievement levels, they will find new, interesting dilemmas that exercise their innovative aptitude.
- **Pushing top performers** to new challenges is the best way to keep these elite assets interested in their work; at the same time it sets the pace for the entire company, as important is the recognition of achievement.
- **Keeping recognition and rewards personal** means sometimes you must step outside of normal recognition and rewards protocol to personalize them so they fit a particular employee's trigger points of commitment. If they are worth the investment, invest.
- **Involve top talent in leadership** sessions early so they feel ownership and pride. This effort keeps you close to new achievers, and you can monitor their growth.

- **Challenge and evaluate** in order to improve communications and expectations. Invest the time to sense signs of migration or unhappiness. Keep a keen eye on projects and ownership that keeps them focused and involved.
- **Promote the culture.** The better your business culture is, the more reasons your best employees will have to stay. Why would they leave when they have their own office, a PA, unlimited tea breaks, and awesome friends at work? Happiness, above all, is the key to retaining staff members.

If you can work these elements into the lives of your best team members, you will improve your retention levels. I've noticed that of all of the incentives, money, recognition, and extras, happiness is still the most important. Job satisfaction is a factor that retains and engages. It does not happen in a vacuum, thus it must be a corporate objective with full attention. These are your moneymakers if they are producing, proving, and reinventing the company as an innovative force within its professional community.

So what exactly is the definition of a top performer? A top performer is someone who is capable of, and interested in, driving the business results you need—someone who will take responsibility for getting results within the parameters of your corporate culture and strategic vision. They work with passion and drive while elevating those around them.

CHAPTER 12

The Anatomy of Innovators

"The creation of something new is not accomplished by the intellect, but by the play instinct arising from inner necessity. The creative mind plays with the object it loves."

CARL JUNG

To get a full understanding of creativity, idea generation, and what makes innovators tick, I will reveal to you the anatomies of how these operate and what is behind their motivations and desires.

We are certainly complex organisms, having individual perspectives that we as managers must somehow generalize and categorize so that we establish and maintain order. Chaos wants to inject itself in each of our efforts, but you must create barriers while allowing for open thought, creative flow, and outside-the-box thinking. This is never an easy task while also maintaining order, compliance, and timeline expectations.

Your perspective is critical in building awareness.

You must awaken the unlimited possibilities that each of your hired staff brings to your company. You have hired them with the expectation that their skills will not just fill space but add value. Conversely, each member of your team is willing and able to make their contribution once they understand the vision, culture, and resources that are available to them.

The Innovative Genes

Imagine your first day on the job. You have already been through the hiring and HR processing gauntlet. You most likely are unaware of the full conditions of your environment, thus you acknowledge you will need a few weeks to assess the playing field before making any big changes or commitments. As a senior level manager and thinker, you are ready to show them what you are made of and begin the process of integrating your DNA into the system. You will call upon your knowledge of what has worked for you before and perhaps use the wisdom of what did not work as part of your toolbox. You possess the desire to achieve great things for yourself and contribute to your new company.

As the CEO responsible for your success, here is what I think I know about you, my new employee:

- **Curious:** Innovation and being a part of a progressive environment is important to you. You are driven by complex issues and get satisfaction from solving dilemmas. You have a 360-degree ability to research, analyze, and solve immediately. You fire on all cylinders because you cannot wait to see what makes your company function and the products that drive revenue, and you are eager to see if your ideas and input will lead to new revenue for the company.

- **Persistent:** You are at the height of your career with several years of experience that has given you the knowledge and wisdom to work at a high-performance pace with grace, calmness, and agility. You are not a retreater or someone who is looking to hide, but rather someone who knows how to deal with adversity while moving your efforts ahead. Adversity in any sense of the word is something that you can navigate with ease, and you can position your agenda in a way that others will follow. You are steady and capable because you have a track record of persevering through tough and good times. You are not intimidated nor are you shaken by controversy. You are focused on moving your team, products, ideas, and efforts to the achievement stage. Profitable growth is your measurement of your effort, and you will not lessen your drive until this is reached.
- **Motivated:** Salary, bonuses, and the benefits that go with being hired are important to you. You are fully aware of your value and that those payments are part of your value to the company. However, you are driven by the fact that you are a professional with an advanced skill set. You are motivated by the need to create and the excitement you will generate by new innovation and discoveries. The opportunity to make changes organizationally and socially through your discoveries is equally or more important to you than your salary and bonuses. If you are not creating something that gets to the market, you are frustrated because you are motivated by the need to finish. That is why you have made the investment in your education, advanced your sense of self, and have continued to pursue self-improvement.
- **Creative:** There are no problems, dilemmas, or adversities that you are unable to overcome. Your creative

sense is part of your decision-making methods. You have the ability to counter each and every problem with a solution that is grounded in solid business acumen. You are not only an owner of your creative asset, but you are a contributor and supporter of others' abilities. Style and grace are inherent to your ability to work the solution backwards to the problem. You are probably able to recite the alphabet backwards without thought as you are connected by your visual and acute ability to overcome obstacles in your mind, teams, or the market. You live in the mindset of an innovator as you are constantly scanning the world for improvements and opportunities.

- **Risk-taker:** You are a risk-taker, who is not reckless but knows when to tap into your visceral business sense for investment. When the analysts, actuaries, accountants, and economists tell you it cannot be done, you know when and how to get the support you need to advance your cause. With different degrees of risk, you are also fully able to correct your course when needed. You know there will be mistakes or new information leading to a new direction, and you are aware of how to fix and take the team with you. Risk reward is a motivator that comes with risk. You are focused on keeping the layers of teams informed and involved. You do not operate in a bubble by yourself; you prepare for contingency, transparency, and communication with any stakeholder involved.

- **Balanced:** You know there has to be a Ying and a Yang to exist fully. It is with humility and passion that you operate with support from all points of your existence. You are aware of pace in keeping yourself grounded while pushing to completion. You are sensitive to which team members work and who does not and are able to make changes quickly so as to restore or establish order.

- **Capable:** Above all other traits is that you are extremely capable. I have hired you because I believe in your ability to serve as a valuable part of our team. I will give you the time and understanding to be successful. I, too, have the attributes mentioned earlier; therefore we will operate with harmonious expectations and hope.

Overall, the perspectives I have illustrated above are to be viewed and imagined by all involved. We must style ourselves for positive perspectives that support the company members and in turn we focus on success while remaining agile to deal with change and outcomes. The perfect people are the ones you've hired.

The Creative Genes – Six Characteristics of Creative People

There are various types of creative influencers in your company. Understanding each type or combinations helps optimize your expectations. Each is motivated differently, thus their desire to contribute needs organic conditions to thrive. These conditions are defined as feedback, involvement, and expectations that fit the style of each. Our aim is to cultivate, train, and internalize the Create Control principles, where we all optimize performance that turns into profitable outcomes.

1: Reflection and Action

In my many years working for different companies, I have found that creative people tend to be secretive about their creativity. The true creative geniuses are not the people who appear to be the most creative or talk about being the most creative. You have to actively look for these traits in people to identify them as highly creative people.

The first trait is reflection and action. Creative people have a never-ending supply of boundless energy, yet they are also quiet and at peace with the world. This is in sharp contrast to people that are restless or are quiet at work because they are introverted.

Highly creative people use their energies in unique ways— perhaps not to run marathons, but they have a knack for iron focus when the occasion demands it. You'll always find that incredibly creative people have the willpower to sit in one place for hours and hours, locked onto the work they're doing, completely absorbed by it.

When they reflect on life, work, and everything else, they can be quiet people. While they are focused on doing something that requires intense concentration, they won't be very talkative, even to the point of being a little rude.

It's not because they aren't social; it's because their creative minds have clicked into gear and are now wholly focused on one thing: their project. Little interruptions such as talking or taking breaks just aren't important anymore.

So, the first trait of highly creative people is that they DO have massive amounts of energy, but they use it differently than people who are busy bodies. Plus they have a calm, reflective disposition sometimes because they're enjoying the moment or are thinking about abstract concepts, life, love, and whatever else inspires them.

If you're look for a highly creative person when you hire someone new, see how they behave at work for the first three months. If they display these traits, you may have found an addition to one of your teams.

2: Smartly Naïve

The second trait of highly creative people has to be that they are smartly naïve about things. For these people, everything and anything is possible. Somehow they have grown up and retained their childlike wonder. There is a real sense of innocence there that just can't be corrupted in any way.

The reason I say these creative people are smart is because they tend to be of above average intelligence. Creativity has been loosely linked to IQ, though experts say that creative genius is its own kind of intelligence that has nothing to do with IQ.

These smart individuals are excellent problem solvers because, despite their education, they have managed to hang on to the ability to think outside the normal cognitive constructs that the education system teaches us.

This is great news for employers who struggle to find people with truly unique perspectives and insights. I'm sure that their creative intelligence also lends itself to their ability to have more insight than the average person, and as you know, this a crucial part of the idea lifecycle.

It's safe to say that smart, naïve, creative people are able to think beyond what normal people can imagine or choose to see. Because of their belief in creativity and their constant naivety about the things that hold most of us back, they are able to see the impossible.

It proves that sometimes "knowing better" doesn't always work better. Because of these traits, highly creative people are prone to increased risk taking—simply because they can see past limitations and the mental constructs and common sense that holds normal people back from attempting similar things.

Combining a smart mind with a naïve approach to what can and can't be done is a lethal combination. It literally makes creative thinkers into innovators, because where we see problems, they see more challenges to overcome.

If you see challenges instead of problems, you're more likely to plunge in and see if you can make your idea a success.

Most people would just decide that the challenge would be too complex, and they'd give up on the idea. That's what separates creative people from your average workers; they never give up before they've tried to make it work.

If you're looking to hire a creative individual, look to see if they display the smart–naïve trait. It will go a long way in helping your creative teams live up to their potential.

3: Disciplined Laziness

The third trait that you need to watch out for is a distinct sense of disciplined laziness that all creative people tend to have. Highly creative people tend to procrastinate when it suits them because it feels natural to mull over an idea for a while.

Unwittingly, they are actually taking part in a crucial part of the idea creation process. I'm talking about allowing ideas to incubate for a while to stimulate those "aha!" moments of insight. It's the reason why a creative person will begin something early and then leave it to the last moment to get it done.

This "laziness" isn't laziness at, all but a strong impulse to let the subconscious mind take part in the idea generation and development process. It's the reason why highly creative people can suddenly come up with flashes of brilliance—even when they seemed to be completely lazy before.

These highly creative people are also fiercely disciplined, with near-superhuman levels of commitment to a project. You'll find that creative types continue to work at home, even if they don't have to. It's because they honestly care about their work, which makes it important to them.

Creative people will sit down and puzzle something out until they are satisfied that they understand it and can use it in the coming days. This sort of discipline is not something you can teach someone. I've had team members who taught themselves entire computer programs in a matter of days because they thought it would benefit the project.

I suppose you could say that these employees are able to combine playfulness and discipline along with responsibility and irresponsibility. There is always a method to their madness, however. While some employees think creative processes are pure fun, the creative individual knows just how much hard work it is, but enjoys it anyway.

If you're looking to hire a creative individual, then look for the disciplined laziness trait. It's easy to spot because your employee will surprise you with their level of dedication and with their apparent inability to stick to a deadline. It's all part of the creative process, and that's something you can't teach—either you have it or you don't.

4: Imagined Reality

The fourth trait of highly creative people is that they are able to alternate between fantasy and reality. These people are usually strongly rooted in reality and yet have an incredible imagination all at the same time.

Because of this dominant trait, creative people will often dream big—and that dream will be detailed and rich. They have the ability to do this for projects as well. If you need to come up with something spectacular that is so complex it's hard to imagine, the highly creative person will be able to see it so clearly that they could draw you a picture.

The ability to imagine alternate realities is one thing, but that's not where the creative person's talent ends. After they have imagined this reality, they can often make it happen by setting goals and working towards an end point.

It's like I said earlier; creativity in its truest form is about creation—whether it's creating a new product or a new reality.

It's all the same for the motivated creative person. This is a very desirable trait for businesses, because it means that their employees will be able to transform concepts into physical, tangible objects.

It's quite rare that people have the motivation, skill, and drive to take something from the concept phase all the way through to the material phase. Creative people do it every day. They visualize what they want, and then they come up with a plan of action so that they can get it. It's the most elegant form of reality creation in the universe!

Imagination is one of those skills that does not mean anything, until you realize how powerful it can be in a team environment. Creative people who have incredible imaginations will be able to sort through problems quicker, find solutions sooner, and see parts of the project as well as the overall end result.

Using their superior imagination skills, these employees will then ensure that all moving parts fit together to create the desired result. It's like planning a list of things to do and then doing them—only the entire process happens in your mind.

Creative people with this trait believe that goals are dreams with a deadline. They are constantly thinking about new and exciting ways to improve their own lives—or your company. Coming up with ideas is their favorite pastime!

If you're searching for a creative person that has the ability to be realistic about products that haven't been created yet, then this is one trait you need. People that are able to imagine desired outcomes and work towards them are innovators, visionaries, and creative geniuses.

You'll notice who these people are because they'll always understand the vision for the project in a very specific way. They'll also be able to work within the parameters you give them—regarding budget, scheduling, and teamwork. This is their realistic side, which fuels their imaginations.

5: Knowledge Sponges

The fifth trait of highly creative people is that they are all knowledge sponges. Because of this, they are not introverted or extroverted but both—whenever the mood strikes them. Creative people tend to live their lives fascinated by knowledge, and they are always willing to learn new things.

This makes them incredibly valuable as employees because they are quick to learn and often have the ability to naturally improve processes to increase their productivity once they have learned something new.

Knowledge sponges can be very introverted, considering the mysteries of who they are and what they want from life. This is why you get many ambitious creative people—they are willing to work hard, learn new things, and better themselves. They follow a plan of action to get to the top of their careers, and they work hard to get there.

These creative types are also very extroverted at times. This allows them to communicate effectively, which is essential for people that love to learn. Not only do they bury themselves in books and the Internet, but they are deeply interested in learning practical applications from people that have more experience than they do.

A creative person that is also a knowledge sponge will be able to learn anything from anyone, which makes them excellent candidates to become managers and leaders. Because they are tuned into learning, knowledge sponges also make great teachers; they are able to listen and are usually more patient than other people.

If you're on the hunt for a creative person that has great leadership potential and will be able to see a project from every angle, then the knowledge sponge is who you need. These creative types are natural-born learners, and they never stop growing as people.

You can take a knowledge sponge from nothing to a junior executive in less than three years. They have an insatiable thirst for knowledge, and they make great mentors for younger staff members. You may also find these knowledgeable types are both conservative and rebellious. They are able to balance their lives very well.

6: Proudly Humble

The final trait that completes the creative individual is that they are proudly humble. All very creative people know how much they are worth because they have an intrinsic sense of self-worth. While these people know what they are capable of achieving, they never boast or brag about their talents.

There is a big difference between being proud of your work and bragging about it. Someone that brags is usually inflating a story that wasn't that impressive in the hope that it will make them seem like something special. Being proud of your achievements, on the other hand, is when you tell others what you have accomplished with no embellishments.

The work and the achievement tend to speak for themselves. These creative types are proud that they spend their time pushing to be better at their jobs. They are always looking for ways to improve themselves, because they enjoy being successful. And there's nothing wrong with a bit of creative ego to give someone confidence in their work.

Having said that, the proudly humble are also very aware of what they are worth—which makes them sensitive to criticism and injustice. If a company, for example, does not recognize their great work or pay them what they deserve, the creative person will leave. This is simply because they know that they are being treated badly and won't stand for it.

It's important to let the proudly humble creative type feel like they are a big part of the team and that everyone appreciates what they do for the company. They need to know that their existence in your company is continually justified. That means awards, congratulations, cash incentives, and acknowledgment need to be dealt liberally.

The proudly humble will never take the credit for something they didn't do, and they don't appreciate false compliments either. Instead, they prefer sincerity and genuine thanks as opposed to fake flattery.

These creative people manage to be proud and humble at the same time, which is a rare gift that is required if you are to be one of the highly creative people in the world. Without modesty, your work will never be taken seriously, which is deeply important to creative types.

And without confidence and pride, creative people would never have the guts to try new things, take risks, and push the boundaries of innovation. You need to ensure that you have a few proud but humble people in your teams. You'll be able to spot them by the way that they acknowledge being acknowledged by others.

If your creative person is slightly embarrassed but very pleased with the compliments, then they have the proud–humble trait. Keep in mind that not all creative people share all of these traits. Sometimes you get creative types who are very egotistical, but it's rare if they are highly creative.

CHAPTER 13

From Theory to Practice

*"In the realm of ideas everything depends on enthusiasm...
in the real world all rests on perseverance."*

JOHANN WOLFGANG VON GOETHE

OK, after all of this great advice, what can you DO to maintain your creative control environment? The answer is to follow an easy to remember systemic process that further helps ensure your goals are being met.

Moving from theory to practice can be tough sometimes, but with the right maintenance techniques, you will begin to stabilize your innovative strategy and creative processes into the company's managerial style. Your team will enjoy the clarity of vision and the thoughtful commitment that ownership in the process will give them.

Devising a Structured Creative Process

The goals of putting a structured creative and innovation process into effect are simple—productivity and results. To make it happen, follow the easy to remember acronym of the "DO IT" principle.

Walt Disney once said, *"If you can dream it, you can do it!"*

DO IT stands for:

Define the problem,
Open your mind,
Identify the solution, and
Transform it into a tangible.

As a means of embodying your problem solving and creative ingenuity in your daily innovative processes, DO IT is easily established as the key to all efforts.

- *Define the Problem:* Get your teams to begin analyzing problems, not symptoms of the problem. Why does the problem exist? Create a framework for the problem by listing your objectives, a break down, and a summary. Defining a problem properly is exactly how you are supposed to begin this creative process.
- *Be Open-minded:* You have got to be open-minded when working with creative techniques so that you can begin to generate effective solutions. Focus on generating as many as you can from your team or pods. Listen to everyone, and share your ideas with everyone. It's an open discussion!
- *Identify the Best Solution:* The next stage of the creative process is to choose the best ideas from your idea pool. Examine and develop a few of the best ideas to see which one stands out the most as the prevailing winner. Make

a decision and then select the appropriate solution. I like using post-it notes with members placing them on the one or two ideas they like best.

- *Transform:* You know what the problem is, and you have a solution to it. The next step is to implement this solution so that the problem is resolved. Develop a reliable product from your idea, and get as much input as you can from your design team.

Creating a Productive Environment

It's not difficult to create a productive working environment, but it does take some planning and execution on your part. The reason why this is so important is that creative people tend to work better in clean, productive environments where they can be left to think and do. Interruptions and other unproductive things can derail their creative process.

Here are some excellent ideas on how to transform your office space into a dynamic and productive working environment:

- *Fix the ambience:* The look and feel of your office certainly affects the way people work. A bland, static environment can actually reduce productivity and lower the mood of your employees. Creative people don't work well if they're not happy. Try adding green plants to the office and warm colors on the walls.
- *Fix the temperature:* Airflow through a building, along with heating and cooling, can significantly affect the productivity of employees. Being too hot or too cold or having a general lack of air in the building destroys job satisfaction. Make sure that your employees are always comfortable in a climate-controlled area.
- *Noise levels:* Everyone knows that a noisy environment is a less productive one, but not always. Keep it quiet where

people work, but allow higher noise levels in break rooms and public areas so that your employees can escape to a place that is different from your work areas.

- *Consider ergonomic design:* Comfort plays its part in productivity, which is why many businesses choose to implement human engineering into their office blocks. This means buying ergonomic chairs and keyboards, which are supposed to rapidly improve productivity because they are so easy to use.

- *Technology:* As a tech company, you will be expected to have the latest technology everywhere, along with some toys that your employees can play with on their breaks. It's not uncommon to see a Nintendo Wii in a break room, and they can actually improve the productivity of the employees who use it.

- *Conflict resolution:* A lot of passionate, creative people in your offices are a potentially disastrous mix. Inevitably there will be personalities that clash and conflicts that will need to be resolved. A big part of having a comfortable, productive working environment is not being exposed to conflict when it arises.

Try implementing these easy fixes if you're struggling to create a harmonious and productive working environment for your creative employees. They will appreciate the changes, and more, it will act as a morale booster. Plus, people will see that changes are happening in your company that is benefiting them.

You can match this physical transformation with the management style transformation and people will accept it more readily. Creativity has come to your company to make things better for everyone!

10 Ways to Boost Creative Productivity

I'm often asked, once all of these processes are in place, how managers can steadily increase creative productivity. In the beginning, it's bound to be fairly slow as people learn the ropes of the new system. That's why you need these tips to get your productivity up and your company earning from their human capital.

1. ***Play with information:*** Once you have established the creative parameters of a job, it's time to mess around with as much information as you can submerge yourself in. You do this to allow for idea incubation.

2. ***Play your ideas:*** Take one idea out of the bunch and play around with it. See how workable it is and if it would work within your predefined parameters. What makes it work or not work? Answer your own battery of questions.

3. ***Don't consider perfection an option:*** When you're playing around with information, ideas, and scenarios, don't allow yourself to be frustrated by the lack of perfection. There is no such thing as perfect, and it just gets in the way of the creative process.

4. ***Encourage breaks:*** This sounds like a strange way to boost creative productivity, but it works. Creative types that daydream and space out at work tend to have better ideas and higher productivity rates.

5. ***Daydream with others:*** Talk to other teams members about your daydream musings. This is a great way to cause that momentary insight that solves all of your problems. It's the reason why daydreamers always have so much time on their hands.

6. ***Do something mindless and repetitive:*** Believe it or not, mindless, repetitive tasks stimulate your subconscious that controls a whopping 96% of your brain. Unleash

your productive side by freeing yourself from barriers with this technique.

7. *Have fun and laugh:* Laughing has been proven to relax the brain, which stimulates creative thought. It just goes to show that when experts tell you to encourage fun in your business, they're doing it for particular reasons!

8. *Snap into focus mode:* Creative people have the ability to click into extreme focus mode, which makes for a highly creative and productive day. Ensure that they have all the ideas and information that they need before they begin.

9. *Separate your tools:* You can train your brain to switch into different modes by using different tools. Using your computer for brainstorming might not be good because your brain is used to typing and working there. Use a notebook to brainstorm instead.

10. *Watch your energy levels:* It's impossible to be creative when your natural stores of energy are depleted, so take care of yourself and get enough sleep. It's also a good idea to eat well and exercise regularly to keep the creativity going.

Use these excellent tips to get your workforce back in action and working at full speed. I like to focus on improving the break areas for my teams; that always increases productivity. It's also a great way to make sure that your innovators are happy in their space.

Relationships and Creativity

There are many ways that you can improve your creative working relationships. I've mentioned before that the way people treat each other in office environments is not conducive to creativity or creative productivity.

People are usually no more than work acquaintances, and they don't know anything about each other—or the lives they live outside of work. It seems like an awful shame, especially because most of your life is spent in a work environment. Do you want your teams to spend most of their lives surrounded by people that don't want to get to know them? No!

Relationships and creativity go hand in hand. Yes, it's been the old mantra to keep your work life and your home life separate, but why? There are good people at work that are worth knowing well, I guarantee it!

Take that first step and tell your teams that things are going to be different from now on. Make an effort to get to know each and every one of your team members on a personal level. You need to do this so that you are adequately prepared to pair them when you need to work on creative projects.

I TOOK ONE OF MY TEAMS TO FENWAY PARK IN BOSTON...

To speak to some of the Red Sox players and management about the dynamics of teamwork and what it means to trust the people you work with. I spoke to the team manager there, who addressed my team, and he spoke at length about emotional involvement being the linchpin that holds a team together.

I know many of my New York colleagues will not agree with me that visiting the Red Sox was the best choice as a team building exercise, but the results were immediate. My staff was psyched to meet some of the best players in baseball and take pictures, and they got to know each other better. This closeness translated into one of the best performing teams.

If you don't know who they are, then you can't play to their strengths or weaknesses. If businesses ran like sports teams, I bet that they would earn far more money and produce far more work. It's because people in sports teams are a solid unit, where everyone works for the benefit of each other.

Improving your work relationships is an essential step in the creative process. In my opinion, you'd be far more creative with trusted colleagues than with total strangers. Because creativity and innovation are now the top commodities in business, there will be more attention to social dynamic. This is a key component to the CREATE System.

Soon, innovation and creative processes with be mandatory course work at all universities. We haven't reached that stage yet, but I am sure it will happen. Once managers see the improvement in team output through ownership and contribution, it will be listed in every job description and expectation. Innovation is a word that is used quite frequently as an end result as opposed to an environmental condition.

Creating Solid Team Dynamics

Building successful teams is really the heart of this creative control process. If you do not have successful creative teams that are fluid and work well together, you are going to struggle to get creativity out of them. Teams are typically united by common goals. It is the glue that creates solid team dynamics. They are highly adaptable and agile.

There are numerous things that can occur within the process of shaping teams. Typically, the best approach for dealing with groups and team dynamics is generally method oriented, using an interpretation of industry standards, management experience, and sometimes the need to try something different. These can be frustrating, as change can be

---

DEFINITION OF FEATURED TEAMS

For a very thorough explanation of "Feature Teams," read the book *"Scaling Lean & Agile Development"* by Craig Larman and Bas Vodde. According to Larman and Vodde, a featured team is a "long lived, cross-functional team that completes many end-to-end customer features, one by one."

---

for many, but gathering the right information, communicating it methodically, and defending processes when needed are all necessary when methods have changed.

Case in Point: Assume for a moment that you have been in charge of implementing an Agile development process at work for a large financial software company. With the help of some other members within Quality Assurance (QA) and your production team, you've finally moved from component-based teams to feature teams. You are now starting to see improvements after making this important systemic change.

However, now management is mandating that you change your team structure again to include something called "pods." The basic idea is based on breaking down the large team into multiple pods, each around a "cluster" of features (e.g., social features, patching features, logging/telemetry features, etc.).

Each pod will still be cross-functional (including QA, developers, production, design, others), but the pods will be semi-static in that they will not be reformed at each release cycle.

Management's explanation for this change is that "this mirrors how things are now done everywhere else in the tech world" and that it will help encourage ownership, knowledge sharing, and career development. The pods will own the features they develop long term, including future maintenance.

Your main counterpoints are:

- This will lead to sub-optimal use of resources. You have been clustering developers with non-orthogonal skill sets into static teams in order to work on features that vary in size and skill set requirements. You are questioning what happens when you have a feature that requires two developers split between different pods.
- Redundancy will lead to a lot of additional management overhead, as teams will not be the right size to accommodate the features and feature estimates.
- You are concerned that you also have to determine how to integrate the work within this additional work structure.

You have a major dilemma that requires you to gather enough information to either position your team appropriately using the new pod method or develop your push back position. To date, you have learned that Agile's best practice is feature teams, you have just established this protocol, and you know nothing about pods. For the sake of your development team, your sanity, and your defense of your own position, you need to get a better understanding why feature teams are the preferred industry-accepted way of working over the pods approach.

You set out to gather more information and learn there is a lot of information on the integration of pods into the Agile method. Your situation is not uncommon, and that alone lets you breathe easier because it is not as detrimental as initially thought.

You have your solution, you present your change strategy to management and your teams, and you begin the process of introducing a new method while keeping your culture tight and engaged. Dynamically, things could have gone wrong on many sides during this scenario. Egos, management conflict, communication techniques, and integration all could have impacted groups and culture. You prevented all this by remembering your DO IT system before engaging in a knee-jerk reaction.

From Ideas to Inventions and Innovations

What makes a team become creative leaders in the field of inventions and innovations? A number of different things! The most important of them all is good leadership. You are the person responsible for the creative control of your team, which makes you the key player in all project outcomes from here on out.

It's up to you to properly train your people to be like the examples you've found in this book and to live up to their potential. Changing ideas into new innovations is not just exciting; it's enthralling for the creative team of ambitious employees.

Seeing their ideas come to life and being sold in the global marketplace will be enough motivation to see it happen again and again. If you implement the creative strategies in this book, you'll find that your team improves with each idea and each product launch.

One day, perhaps a year from now, you'll look back at the training and hard work and say it was all worth it. And that's because you'll have a creative product on the market that has literally made your company a fortune. That's the ultimate goal.

To get there is going to take hard work and dedication on your part from the beginning—right up until you hand your team over to another manager. Prepare a training manual for your teams that will teach them everything you've learned in this book, or simply make this book prescribed reading for work.

Ideas are a dime a dozen; any great business person will tell you that. What separates the thriving businesses and teams from the rest is the execution of these ideas. Now that you've learned about the creative process, you can use it to leverage ideas and transform them into usable, practical, and desirable products for the open market.

Your teams will become like pillars—lifting your company up to greater heights. To get to the point where innovation is possible, you simply must focus on your team dynamics. Right now they are barely work friends. With a bit of a push, they can become the best team of innovators your company has ever seen.

Don't forget to inspire your people whenever you can with the work that you do and the things that you teach them. To be a creative leader is to be a compassionate one. Never forget how hard it's been to reach this point in your career where you can blaze new trails in your company to leverage a desired commodity such as creativity.

Once upon a time there were people helping you and training you. Become a student of creativity and place it at the core of your business culture as well. I can't stress to you enough how important it is to continue the idea lifecycle if you want to succeed.

There will be times when you feel disillusioned, but push through them! Nothing worth doing has ever come easily. Train your teams. Change your company. Make the difference in your company's bottom line and be the hero!

CHAPTER 14

Sustaining the Innovative Environment

"Listen to anyone with an original idea, no matter how absurd it may sound at first. If you put fences around people, you get sheep. Give people the room they need."

WILLIAM MCKNIGHT, 3M PRESIDENT

Environment plays an important part in developing our creative outlet and helps shape our innovative expression. On a recent visit and drive from Barcelona, Spain, along the Costa Brava north through France's Mediterranean coast and into Italy, I was struck by the amazing beauty that I had previously only read about and seen in pictures. It is breathtaking and blatantly obvious why so many artists of all sorts have escaped to that place for inspiration. It inspires the senses. From its grandeur of colors to the texture of its terrain, it just puts you in a creative mindset.

Massachusetts Institute of Technology's famous Media Lab is such a place when it comes to inspiring creativity and expanding innovative concepts. "Inventing a better future" is the theme of the Media Lab's work, and you feel inspired by just being in its presence. The Media Lab works as a springboard for innovation and creative thinking for students, entrepreneurs, inventors, corporations, and academics.

It is set up for all kinds of environmental benefits, such as transferring knowledge, sharing prototype or idea demonstrations, allowing for cross-collaboration among different companies and sometime competitors, and is and has been the catalyst for many start-up companies and products. This, not unlike a church is a place to inspire worship, is a place to focus your imagination and ingenuity.

One of my graduate school technology instructors, David Rose from the Graduate Center of Marlboro College, started a successful company from the inspiration of the Media Lab, called Ambient Devices. Their products integrate personal and meaningful data information, in real-time, to useful illuminating devices. Colored illuminations is as big a part of the invention as color, and what the color has been programmed to mean is a quick and visual display as an alert from a pre-defined data feed by the customer. For example, if a pre-programmed stock is tracking well, the device illuminates green. Conversely, if your stock or the entire portfolio is doing poorly, it turns orange and then red. This can be used for any set of conditions. A friend bought one of their Orbs (a small globe) that changes color based on ecommerce sales his company tracks in real-time. In a sense, it does what a clock does with time but with personalized data. Brilliant!

There are hundreds of successful companies such as Ambient Devices that originated out of the Media Lab. It is set up to improve the odds of success. Your company is also an incubator for success and could greatly improve its processes, creativity, and innovative output with your renewed commitment for perfect innovation. There is nothing stopping you from having a mini MIT-type Media Lab in your company.

So, what is it that creative and innovative cultures have that you need? Is it knowledge transfer, generous benefactors, a creative look and feel, or a differentiating culture from every place else your staff has worked previously?

People are used to a certain set of standards and, to some degrees, like predictability. They do not expect deviance or chaos, but know these too are good in small doses to invigorate the creative juices.

I have always liked Sam Harrison's perspectives on idea generation. The author of *Idea Selling* articulates the potential outcomes for creative ideas falling into one of these hazardous categories:

- **Tombstone:** All ideas dead and buried within 24 hours
- **Piñata:** Hold up an idea and watch it get whacked to bits
- **Fish Market:** Bosses stare at ideas with eyes like dead fish.
- **Déjà Vu:** "We've always done it this way, so do it this way again."

Your objective as the engineer of your innovative culture is to never allow these to happen.

A company such as IDEO's main commodity is tapping into the creativity and ingenuity of its employees. That is what they are known for and what they deliver for their customers. They are like an innovation factory, turning out impressive solutions. This is not to suggest a lack of customization, as they have a high degree of expectations on the type of people they hire and their contribution to unique innovation on every assignment.

Big names call on IDEO for small design changes that can have large impacts on the consumer relationship with a product, or they are called to help develop large-scale innovations for such companies as Samsung, Procter & Gamble, Kraft, and Pepsi, to name a few.

The environmental structure of IDEO[17] encourages the use of portable furniture. This encourages employees to travel around the office and compare ideas with other team members. To the outside world this would be seen as chaotic, but this is the best environment for collaborations.

The company also relies on collaborative brainstorming to sustain its idea generation. In this instant, each employee is given an area to research on a particular problem. At the end of the first day of planning, they report back to the group with their ideas. They provide rough sketches and ideas. All ideas are then reviewed by all of the team. A kind of voting method is used to endorse and rule out some ideas. The number of post-it notes placed on a sketch by team members indicates the favorite idea. It is usually the favorite ideas that become the building blocks for prototypes. The team works together to compile the popular ideas and decide how best they could be utilized. Quickly these ideas become the designs of a new prototype for the client to review.

Understanding Influences

What we, as senior managers, have observed and learned from working in various companies is that some teams, pods, people, and bosses can have both positive and negative impacts on our behavior. Your ability to recognize these potential influencers can serve as antidotes to adverse reactions.

---

17   http://www.cbsnews.com/video/watch/?id=50138327n

Individuals vs. Group Environments

Working with an individual is different from working with groups, but it doesn't mean that the principles are different when you're trying to encourage creativity in the workplace. Whether you're trying to unlock the potential inside one person or several hundred as part of a multinational corporation strategy, the same principles apply.

What Is a Creative Environment Like?

- Your ideas matter and are evaluated, no matter what your job description says.
- There is an open platform for suggestion to other teams.
- When you offer new ideas, the managers make you feel appreciated.
- You are celebrated for who you are and what you can do.
- There is always someone waiting to hear your ideas.
- Managers teach and help you, giving you all the details of your projects.
- Trying new things and taking risks is encouraged.
- There is no strict hierarchy in place; you can speak to people freely.
- You are not policed by overbearing bosses.
- You are allowed to work in your own way.
- You feel like you are equal to everyone, even your bosses.
- You are rewarded for good ideas and hard work.
- You are always treated with respect as a valuable team member.

This should give you a good idea about what a creative environment is like for employees. Now, to sustain this for individuals and groups is going to take an enormous amount of hard work, but it's very worth it in the end.

When you show your employees that you care about your company and the people inside your company, they will be willing to help you maintain a creative environment. That's the beauty of transforming the traditional structure into a creative one—everyone is there to pull their weight and make a difference.

Launch an initiative called the "Creativity Now" initiative, and get everyone involved. Use this book to teach others about the power of creativity and what creative control can give to your company. Once they see the evidence of the Creative Control process, they will be sold on the program!

Changing Company Behavior

There are so many great tips that come to mind when I think about teaching you how to change the way people behave in your company. Just know that it starts with you. If people see that you are serious about the change, they will become serious about it as well.

Here are some excellent tips that I have collected over the years:

- First understand people, then try to be understood.
- Don't be afraid to seek the opinions of your employees; it builds confidence and respect between you.
- Don't ever criticize or judge other people's ideas, or they won't share them with you.
- Don't ever claim someone else's idea as you own, even if it's a small one.
- Launch an initiative for company creativity and distribute leaflets.
- Train all of your staff to become more creative with what they do.

- Realize that behavioral shifts don't happen overnight, and they never end.
- Change your meeting structures to invite creative expression.
- Discuss corporate strategy with people who don't make the decisions in your company.
- Keep an ongoing list of problems and improvement areas.
- Reward the people who take to your new processes.
- Reward people when they go the extra mile during the creative process.
- Invite people to challenge your ideas, and don't take it personally when they do.
- Don't stop learning about creativity or how to improve other people's creativity.
- Organize training exercises for your employees that promote creativity.
- If something very creative becomes successful, host workshops to discuss it.
- Be flexible with your employees, and thank them for making the effort.

As you can tell from this list, changing company behavior happens one action at a time. In a number of small ways, this can all add up to a total shift for your business. If you play your cards right, within a few months these practices will become the norm. Your old hierarchical structure will be gone, and communication lines will be opened up.

Continually gather feedback from your teams on how you can better change company behavior for everyone. They will become very interested and will offer you a lot of great suggestions. People love to be part of something important, so make this important, and it will spread through your company.

IT'S TRUE THAT COMPANY BEHAVIOR CAN BE CHANGED...

But don't expect it to change instantly or all at once. Some people will invite creativity into the workplace; others will view it with disdain, as if it's extra work for them to do.

But you have led the charge in the fight against a stifling environment. Be the dynamic, creative manager who inspires others to also be that way. If you locate some negative parties, pull them aside and speak to them about spreading negativity about the new initiative. It will help others at least try the new program.

The Principles of Sustaining Creativity

There are many sound principles for sustaining creativity in a working environment. Here are a few I've picked up along the way:

1. Every employee should understand your company's mission and goals and should be charged with making these a reality.
2. Get rid of micro-management and start to trust your employees on all levels. They will eventually manage themselves, as people tend to do when they're trusted.
3. Get your team members excited about demonstrating the commitment that they have to creativity and innovation in the workplace.
4. Always communicate with enthusiasm and share the lessons that you've learned with your team. Learn from their lessons as well, if they want to share.

5. Train your employees to think like the creative people that they are. They'll discover the power of creative thinking and how it improves their work processes.

6. Supply your employees with whatever they need to be creative—money, methods, materials, more people, and motivation.

7. Create a creative, dynamic working environment that encourages trust and commitment across departments, job descriptions, and projects.

8. Innovation begins when people take an active role in converting problems into ideas. Make the workplace a great environment for asking and answering questions.

9. Colocation can result in change or better relationships. Put people together more often, and it will stimulate creative thoughts.

10. Different is good, sometimes better. In this world of innovation, the best is often the most different, weird, strange, or alternative. Look out for people that have a knack for being original.

These ten principles for sustaining creativity in the working environment are just the tip of the iceberg. There are many other principles that you could apply that would help make creativity a crucial part of your business.

It's also a good idea to become an expert at inspiring others. It's not always easy to be creative when you're not inclined that way. To get creativity out of your people, you'll sometimes have to reach down deep, and inspire them with your words or deeds.

Remember to be the "idea support" that your employees need. This means encouraging them to take risks, to invest themselves in "idea" time, and to recognize and reward them when they do truly achieve something great. Work environments don't have to be stiff and boring; they can also be inspiring and fun.

On the whole, companies that promote a culture of hard work and fun together are the ones that attract the best minds. The only way you're going to get creativity is if you release your employees from their hierarchy.

William McKnight once said, *"If you put fences around people, you get sheep."* Equally, it is how people are made to feel more than what is said to them.

CREATE – Start Now!

The moment you close this book, it is time to organize a meeting with your management team to discuss how you will turn your company into a new creative and innovative hub. You will express a sense of urgency for implementing the CREATE System of **C**onceptualize, **R**elate, **E**mbody, **A**ctualize, **T**riumph, and **E**vangelize into the company culture immediately.

You will focus on the important outcomes for creating your high output, high impact, and high performance individuals across your enterprise. Remember, these six elements are the core of CREATE, which will lead you to the actualization of your innovation principle:

- Improved employee contribution at all levels of your company
- A company that has an organic reputation for quality
- An environment where all feel ownership in every aspect of your business
- The desire and drive to achieve excellence within all of your people
- Market differentiation for your business
- Complete control of the company's creative control environment

Once you embed the six CREATE steps, you will have fulfilled the promise you have made to your company and its stakeholders. You realize you must follow each of these critical steps in order to fully actualize your new innovative environment. You will soon see the benefits of your investment through the new collective attitude of your people and, ultimately, new differentiating revenues.

Step 1: Conceptualization

This is the foundation to exercising, expanding, and developing the scope of your intention. When conceptualizing a new idea, it is essential to direct the thinking to the framework questions and gather answers to help evolve the idea through the various stages of its lifecycle. Impacts on developing your solutions include your environment and market overlapped with the strategic vision of your company.

Your top conceptualizers will focus their process on the strategic vision and the business model it supports by committing to these four phases:

Phase I.   Concise understanding for the strategic vision
Phase II.   Business model alignment
Phase III.   Differentiation (ours and theirs)
Phase IV.   Complexity (costs and time)

Step 2: Relate

The second stage is to **R**elate your idea to all things internal and external. That means establishing logical or causal connections between your idea and your team's ideas and beginning to form a relationship with the rest of the economic world. It becomes an internal–external or inside-out relationship that must become symbiotic in a natural and organic way. The relationship between your creativity and innovations is symbiotic, as they are complementary partners.

Step 3: Embodiment

The third stage is to make sure that your ideas embody your proposed vision, goals, elements, and actions. To embody something means to make it "concrete" or perceptible to others.

Step 4: Actualize

The fourth stage is to **A**ctualize your idea by physically creating it and by making it real! You will understand the motivation factors that help your teams and individuals assimilate the true meaning of actualization and how that produces the best ideas, ingenuity, and differentiating innovation.

Step 5: Triumph

The fifth stage is to **T**riumph over adversity and your competitors by continually developing your creative control environment. The process by which you and your teams have overcome all the challenges, expected and unexpected, is an amazing accomplishment. Whether the new innovation is new to you, to your industry, or to competitors, it needs to be recognized as an event. It is part of your creative commitment to acknowledge and celebrate all accomplishments that lead to product innovation. You are committed to your team, as they are the catalyst for accomplishments. Show them the love and appreciation, and it will come back to you ten-fold.

Step 6: Evangelize

The final part of the CREATE System is to **E**vangelize new initiatives, products, innovation, and your overall company. This means to completely embody your commitment to your innovation strategy by promoting, living, and celebrating every activity within your company. You will use customer evangelism as a way of capitalizing on the success of your products that are successfully used by your core customer base. Company and product evangelism make it possible for total corporate objectives to be met because it forms a basis for all other objectives to be met. Your company is now on its way to full actuality of its strategic mission.

You and your entire company have the ability to apply the **CREATE System** at any time, start again, and reload when needed. As a system, I have designed it to be a never-ending circle of improvement—gradually increasing your creative potential until your company is creating the best products in their class.

At the end of the day, you want creative people in a creative environment—creating new innovations for your company. This is the ideal that you need to work towards if you want to experience a true change in progress.

Becoming a CREATE Ambassador

Becoming someone who is excellent at creatively controlling the people in your business is the reason why you bought this book. By now, you've realized just how much work you have ahead of you. The good news is that once you have implemented the strategies in this book, you will begin to transform into a CREATE ambassador.

You're already partly there, because you've taken the time to learn what you need to do to make your people and your company a better place. If at any time you feel like you're lost and you're not sure if you're doing the right thing creatively, remember that sometimes the biggest discoveries come from the greatest mistakes.

In the world of creativity and innovation, there is no wrong way. Sure, you can leave things as they are and risk being dominated by a creative competitor, but that's just not worth it. Right now you know two things—your business is not creative enough, and you could be doing a lot better as a company.

Reading this book was a great first step into a new skill set for you. With the rise of technology and the boom in creativity as the dominant commodity these days, companies everywhere will soon have to do all they can with their workforces to stay relevant. Managers who do not learn to adapt will not survive.

Think about what you've learned as you guide your company through the various phases of CREATE. There are so many ways to be better and to make a real difference in your company. I believe that mastering and sharing this process is the most effective managerial technique that you can learn today.

I've spent years trying to hone in on what it is that makes good teams work and others fail—when they had all the potential in the world to be great. Creativity is one of those intangible things that can be encouraged, but without a lot of hard work and effort, it will never be mastered.

You are now the person in your company who has opened this door for new ingenuity and innovation. You are the person who turns it all around and changes the business culture into something all can be proud of.

You may never realize how much of a difference you can make to the reputation and bottom line of your company with these creative techniques. And it makes even more of an impact on your employees. They begin to enjoy work again, and they really push themselves to produce quality, creative work for you. That's what creative control is all about!

Conclusion

If this book has inspired you, at the least, to rethink your priorities and place innovation and your creative assets at the head of your strategic vision, then I have met my objective. At that most, I am hoping you will assemble your brain trust immediately and start the process of improving and controlling your company's entire innovative environment. This book is filled with tools to get you started and tactics to maintain your program. It is in the best interests of your knowledge workers, your entire stakeholder population, and your contribution to the technology community, for which you operate, to fulfill your commitment as a high performance example.

I believe it is time to leverage the best of yourself, your staff, and your company resources to create a differentiating enterprise that is sustaining and satisfying as a place to create, innovate, and inspire.

Companies and countries are at their best when they are built on the foundation of the innovative spirit. Pride resonates throughout all of us when we have performed at our very best and have the empirical evidence to show for it. It is about making a difference through contribution and collaboration that allows us to learn from each lesson and grow. We are no longer affected by others' influences or environmental constraints due to our own wisdom. You and your teams are able to tap into each other's creative sense to control and apply ingenuity in any situation, at any time and any place.

Creativity in a business context is about sourcing original ideas from your workforce, developing new approaches to problems, taking risks, and contributing something to the business that has real value. Innovation in a business context is about turning those high performance ideas into tangible, profitable products.

Take this opportunity now to approach work with a new sense of purpose and a fresh perspective to share with your company. New possibilities are on the horizon for you and your company; you only needed to take that first crucial step, which you have already done. Before you know it, people will be approaching you and asking all about the Creative Control process. Don't keep it a secret—share it!

Learning how to control creativity will improve your life and the lives of those around you!

- Brian W. Bickford

References

A Model of The Creative Process, http://www.dubberly.com/concept-maps/creative-process.html

Gilkey, Charlie, *Demystifying The Creative Process*, http://www.productiveflourishing.com/demystifying-the-creative-process/

Root-Bernstein, Michele and Robert, *Imagine That! Teaching The Creative Process*, http://www.psychologytoday.com/blog/imagine/201105/teaching-the-creative-process

Chapter 1

Quotes on Creativity and Innovation, Leading Thoughts, http://www.leadershipnow.com/creativityquotes.html

Girotra, Karan, Terwiesch, Christian, Ulrich, Karl, *Faculty & Research Working Paper*, Idea Generation and The Quality of The best Idea, http://www.insead.edu/facultyresearch/research/doc.cfm?did=42236

Bollier, David, *The Future of Creative Control in The Digital Age*, http://www.learcenter.org/pdf/CreativeControl.pdf

Garrett, Chris, *Leveraging Authority For Creative Control, Freedom and Rewards*, http://www.chrisg.com/creative-control/

The Key To Creativity: Solitude or Teams? http://www.nytimes.com/2012/01/19/opinion/the-key-to-creativity-solitude-or-teams.html?_r=0

Boches, Edward, *10 Rules For Modern Collaboration*, http://edwardboches.com/10-rules-for-modern-collaboration

Chapter 2

Quotes on Creativity and Innovation, http://www.leadershipnow.com/creativityquotes.html

Breen, Bill, *The 6 Myths of Creativity,* http://www.fastcompany.com/51559/6-myths-creativity

Creativity in Small Groups, http://www.mhhe.com/socscience/comm/group/students/creativity.htm

Bright Ideas: The Creative Power of Groups, http://hbswk.hbs.edu/item/1041.html

Glimpse Into a Group Creative Process, http://beingmusicalbeinghuman.com/2011/04/17/glimpse-into-a-group-creative-process/

Uzzi, Brian, *Collaboration and Creativity: The Small World Problem,* http://www.kellogg.northwestern.edu/faculty/uzzi/ftp/uzzi's_research_papers/uzzi&spiroajs_smallworlds.pdf

Find Your Inner Creativity, http://visionandwords.com/tag/inspire-creativity/

Chapter 3

Quotations: Creativity and Innovation in the Workplace, http://www.creativityatwork.com/quotes-creativity-innovation-workplace/#.UPsTpW_296w

Seidel, Stefan, *How Does Creativity Impact Business Processes?* http://is2.lse.ac.uk/asp/aspecis/20080143.pdf

Genius, Creativity and Talent – Psychology, psychology.ucdavis.edu/Simonton/GeniusCreativityTalent.ppt

Chapter 4

Creativity Quotes, http://www.brainyquote.com/quotes/keywords/creativity.html

What Inspires Creativity In The Workplace?, http://www.bloomberg. com/video/what-inspires-creativity-in-the-workplace-xLy2z9V~TGKtienzTsGryQ.html

Sloane, Paul, *Does Encouraging Creativity in The Workplace Improve Innovation?* http://www.innovationmanagement.se/2012/11/09/ does-encouraging-creativity-in-the-workplace-improve-innovation/

Creativity at Work, http://www.unfortu.net/~rafe/links/creativity.htm

Dunstan, Wendy, *Creativity and The Workplace*, http://www. thecoachinginstitute.com.au/creativity-and-workplace

Chapter 5

Jobs, Steve, BrainyQuote, http://www.brainyquote.com/quotes/ quotes/s/stevejobs416925.html

4 Lessons In Creativity From John Cleese, http://www.fastcocreate. com/1680999/4-lessons-in-creativity-from-john-cleese

Frost, Shelley, *How To Align Employees With Company Goals*, http:// smallbusiness.chron.com/align-employees-company-goals-11667.html

The Incredible Power of Company-Wide Goal Alignment and Organizational Business Goals, https://www.successfactors.com/ en_us/lp/articles/corporate-goal-alignment.html

Bloom, David, *Matching Individual Goals To Company Objective Crux of Successful Bonus Plan*, http://www.independent.ie/business/small-business/matching-individual-goals-to-company-objectives-crux-of-successful-bonus-plan-2444705.html

Creating Inclusive and Harmonious Workplaces, http://www.mom.gov. sg/Documents/employment-practices/WDM/Managers_Guide.pdf

Chapter 6

Nikola Tesla Quotes, http://thinkexist.com/quotation/i_do_not_ think_there_is_any_thrill_that_can_go/217139.html

Batey, Mark, *Creativity is The Key Skill For The 21ˢᵗ Century*, http://www.creativitypost.com/business/creativity_is_the_key_skill_for_the_21st_century

Hill: Creativity Offers Mankind's Best Hope in an Uncertain Future, http://one.arch.tamu.edu/news/2012/12/6/hill-future/

Ellerman, Elise, *Creativity is the Currency of The Future*, http://www.kindynews.com/1/post/2012/07/creativity-is-the-currency-of-the-future.html

Creativity and Innovation: Today's Sought-After Commodities, http://www.2sbdigest.com/innovation-process*

Chapter 7

50 Awesome Quotes on The Power of Ideas, http://www.ideachampions.com/weblogs/archives/2010/11/50_very_awesome.shtml

Loewenstein, Jeffrey, Cronin, Matthew, *The Creative Cycle*, https://server1.tepper.cmu.edu/Seminars/docs/Org%20Sci%20PROP%20Final.pdf

Rock, David, Your Brain at Work, http://www.psychologytoday.com/blog/your-brain-work/201009/how-have-more-insights

Moore, Richard, *The Lifecycle of Creative Endeavors*, http://quaylargo.com/rkm/EM/feb97EGCreativity.shtml

Unger, Sarah, The Idea Lifecycle, http://www.holmesreport.com/opinion-info/12785/The-Idea-Lifecycle.aspx

Cooke, Brian, *Lesson Four: Creativity and The Business Life Cycle*, http://irislearning.squarespace.com/storage/2154-L4.pdf

Chapter 8

Milken, Lowell, *Quotes Human Capital*, http://lowellmilken.com/Lowell-milken-quotes/human-capital/

Rock, Dr. David, *Your Brain at Work*, http://www.psychologytoday.com/blog/your-brain-work/201009/how-have-more-insights

People: Your Most Important Corporate Asset, http://www.impactsafety.
org/violencewhitepaper1.htm

Fawcett, Max, *Why People Really Are Your Company's Most Important
Asset*, http://albertaventure.com/2013/01/why-people-really-are-
your-companys-most-important-asset/

Schutt, Florian, *The Importance of Human Capital For Economic
Growth*, http://www.iwim.uni-bremen.de/publikationen/pdf/W027.
pdf

McGunagle, Doreen, *Human Capital Importance in an Organization*,
http://www.globalstrategicmgmt.com/blog/bid/81326/Human-
Capital-Importance-in-an-Organization

Human Capital, Investopedia, http://www.investopedia.com/
terms/h/humancapital.asp#axzz2IO0duz1o

The Importance of Human Capital in Business, http://www.slideshare.
net/FBBProject/the-importance-of-human-capital-in-business

Highhouse, Scott, *Measuring Attraction To Organizations*, http://
users.ugent.be/~flievens/attraction.pdf

How Monetary Rewards Can Demotivate Creative Works, http://
www.techdirt.com/articles/20100603/0311539672.shtml

Banks, Bonnie, Winston, Bruce, *The Importance of Creativity
and Innovation in Organizations*, http://www.leadingtoday.org/
Onmag/2008%20Archives/November%2008/bb-november08.pdf

Do Hierarchies Help or Hinder Innovation? http://firmfollowsform.
com/?p=89

Moore, Karl, Hill, Kyle, *The Decline But Not Fall of Hierarchy –
What Young People Really Want*, http://www.forbes.com/sites/
karlmoore/2011/06/14/the-decline-but-not-fall-of-hierarchy-
what-young-people-really-want/

To Nurture Business Creativity, Try Equality, http://inequality.org/
nurture-business-creativity-equality/

Suttle, Rick, *How To Treat Employees With Respect To Increase Productivity*, http://smallbusiness.chron.com/treat-employees-respect-increase-productivity-31072.html

Chapter 9

15 Awesome Quotes on Collaboration, http://www.ideachampions.com/weblogs/archives/2010/07/35_awesome_quot.shtml

Loewenstein, Jeffrey, Cronin, Matthew, *The Creative Cycle*, https://server1.tepper.cmu.edu/Seminars/docs/Org%20Sci%20PROP%20Final.pdf

Product Development: 9 Steps For Creative Problem Solving [INFOGRAPHIC], http://mashable.com/2011/09/30/creative-problem-solving/

What is Creative Problem Solving? http://www.creativeeducationfoundation.org/our-process/what-is-cps

Rietzschel, Eric, Nijstad, Bernard, Stroebe, Wolfgang, *The Selection of Creative Ideas After Individual Idea Generation: Choosing Between Creativity and Impact*, http://personal.stevens.edu/~rchen/creativity/idea%20selection.pdf

Chapter 10

Creativity Quotes, http://www.notable-quotes.com/c/creativity_quotes.html

Seven Stages of The Creative Process, http://www.mgtaylor.com/mgtaylor/glasbead/7stagcrp.htm

Ferlic, K, *The Creative Process*, http://ryuc.info/common/creation_process/creative_process.htm

Milbourn, Tad, *How Do You Merge Ideas*, http://support.intuitbrainstorm.com/entries/212365-how-do-you-merge-ideas

Wallis' Model of The Creative Process, http://members.optusnet.com.au/charles57/Creative/Brain/wallis.htm

What It Really Takes To Turn an Idea Into Reality, http://www.smh.com.au/small-business/managing/blogs/enterprise/what-it-really-takes-to-turn-an-idea-into-reality-20121004-270lv.html

How Unusual Combinations Lead To Breakthrough Ideas, http://www.innovationmanagement.se/imtool-articles/how-unusual-combinations-lead-to-breakthrough-ideas/

Sugars, Brad, *How Can I Turn an Idea into Reality Without Any Business Savvy?* http://www.entrepreneur.com/answer/222115

How To Turn The Greatest Idea Ever Into Reality, http://www.instigatorblog.com/how-to-turn-the-greatest-idea-ever-into-reality/2006/09/19/

Chapter 11

Ideas Quotes, http://www.brainyquote.com/quotes/keywords/ideas.html

Marmolejo, Nancy, *How To Monetize Your Creativity: 4 Tips For Entrepreneurs*, http://www.brandstyledesign.com/2012/03/how-to-monetize-your-creativity-4-tips-for-entrepreneurs/

How To Get Your Creativity To Pay Off In Your Business, http://vivavisibilityblog.com/creativity-payoff/

Hiring The Right Candidates For an Offshore Team, http://www.flatworldsolutions.com/articles/hiring-the-right-candidate.php

Heathfield, Susan, *10 Tips For Hiring The Right Employee*, http://humanresources.about.com/od/recruiting/tp/recruiting_employee.htm

Browning, Geil, *How To Spot Innovative Hires*, http://www.inc.com/geil-browning/how-to-identify-innovative-new-hires.html

Safko, Lon, *The Three C's of Innovative Thinking*, http://www.ftpress.com/articles/article.aspx?p=765246

7 Habits of Highly Innovative People, http://thinksimplenow.com/creativity/7-habits-of-highly-innovative-people/

Lomenick, Brad, *18 Rules For Creative Meetings*, http://www. bradlomenick.com/2011/11/01/18-rules-for-creative-meetings/

Hiring and Retaining Good Employees: Crucial Strategies For Success, http://www.wolfgugler.com/docs/hiringandretaining.pdf

How To Find a Million Dollar Business Idea (In Minutes), http://www. forbes.com/sites/theyec/2012/09/28/how-to-find-a-million-dollar-business-idea-in-minutes/

Seven Tips For Keeping Your Best Creative Talent, http://www.aquent. com/blog/seven-tips-for-keeping-your-best-creative-talent

9 Steps To Attracting and Retaining Creative Talent, http://www. thelookinglass.com/white-papers/9-steps-to-attracting-and-retaining-creative-talent.html

Chapter 12

Mathers, Alex, *25 inspiring Quotes For Creative People*, http://www. redlemonclub.com/brand-you/25-inspiring-quotes-for-creative-people/

Wasu, Shalu, *16 Habits of Highly Creative People*, http://tickledbylife. com/index.php/16-habits-of-highly-creative-people/

Uri, The 10 Habits of Highly Creative People, Applied To Creative Companies, http://www.thecrossedcow.com/2012/04/27/creative-people-creative-companies/

Naiman, Linda, *Seven Habits of Highly Creative People*, http:// di-smith.blogspot.com/2012/11/seven-habits-of-highly-creative-people.html

Chapter 13

Ideas Quotes, http://www.brainyquote.com/quotes/keywords/ideas.html

Do It, A Simple Process For Creativity, http://www.mindtools.com/ pages/article/newCT_09.htm

Top 10 Ways To Create a More Focused and Productive Work Environment, http://lifehacker.com/5866866/top-10-ways-to-create-a-more-focused-and-productive-work-environment

How To Create a Productive Working Environment, http://blog.rockthepost.com/2012/03/how-to-create-a-productive-working-environment/

Fields, Jonathan, *7 Ways To Enhance Focus, Creativity, Productivity and Performance*, http://www.psychologytoday.com/blog/awake-the-wheel/201005/7-ways-enhance-focus-creativity-productivity-and-performance

Hammond, Darell, *How To Boost Creativity, Productivity and Morale in The Workplace: Let Your Employees Play!*, http://www.huffingtonpost.com/darell-hammond/how-to-boost-creativity-p_b_523069.html

Jacobs, Denise, *Four Secrets To Enhancing Creative Productivity*, http://www.netmagazine.com/features/four-secrets-enhancing-creative-productivity

Forman, Leslie, *How To Improve Your Creativity and Productivity*, http://www.learnvest.com/2012/12/how-to-improve-your-creativity-and-productivity/

Forces That Drive Team Dynamics, http://www.studymode.com/essays/Forces-Drive-Team-Dynamics-97081.html

Team Dynamics, Part 2: Building Successful Teams, http://www.cpehr.com/blog/team-dynamics-part-ii-building-successful-teams.html

Chapter 14

Inspire Creativity & Innovation In The Workplace, http://www.creativityatwork.com/quotes-creativity-innovation-workplace/#.UPkh62_296w

How To Sustain Organizational Success Through Creative Thinking – A Seven Step Model, http://www.drakepulse.com/2012/07/how-to-sustain-organizational-success-through-creative-thinking-a-seven-step-model/

Creating a Creative Environment For Brainstorming, http://www.brainstorming.co.uk/tutorials/creativeenvironment.html

The Essence of Innovation: 5 Principles, http://www.ccl.org/leadership/podcast/transcript5Principles.aspx

Paris, Anne, *A New Approach To Igniting and Sustaining Creativity*, http://www.dreammanifesto.com/approach-igniting-sustaining-creativity-2.html

Baumgartner, Jeffrey, *10 Steps For Boosting Creativity*, http://www.jpb.com/creative/creative.php

10 Steps To Be More Creative, and Why Ideas Matter More Than Ever, http://shakeoffthegrind.com/productivity/10-steps-to-being-more-creative-and-why-ideas-matter-more-than-ever

Ray, Michael, *Creativity in Business*, http://www.ideatribe.com/coaching/Creativity_in_Bus_Overview.pdf

Additional References

Poh, Michael, *6 Ways To Unleash Creativity in The Workplace*, http://www.hongkiat.com/blog/unleash-creativity-workplace/

Imagine That: Fostering Creativity In The Workplace, http://www.npr.org/2012/03/21/148607182/fostering-creativity-and-imagination-in-the-workplace

Fries, Amy, *Sparking Creativity in The Workplace*, http://www.psychologytoday.com/blog/the-power-daydreaming/201002/sparking-creativity-in-the-workplace

Foster a Culture of Creativity in Your Workplace, http://www.
allbusiness.com/human-resources/employee-development-
problem-solving/2974875-1.html#axzz2EEP0bDI7

Naiman, Linda, *Creativity at Work Newsletter*, http://www.
creativityatwork.com/2010/03/31/creativity-at-work-newsletter-
fostering-creativity-in-the-workplace/

Kerr, Michael, *25 Ways To Keep Ideas Flowing in Your
Workplaces*, http://www.mikekerr.com/humour-resources/
free-articles/putting-creativity-to-work-articles/25-ways-to-
keep-ideas-flowing-in-your-workplaces/

Chong, E., & Ma, X. (2010). The influence of individual factors,
supervision and work environment on creative self-efficacy.
Creativity And Innovation Management, 19(3), 233-247.
doi:10.1111/j.1467-8691.2010.

Fera, R. A. (2012, June 28). 4 lessons in creativity from John Cleese.
Fast Company, Co. CREATE.

Jaruzelski, B. & Katzenbach, J. (2012). Building a Culture That
Energizes Innovation. Financial Executive, 28(2), 32-35. http://
www.financialexecutives.org/KenticoCMS/Financial-Executive-
Magazine/2012_03/Building-a-Culture-That-Energizes-
Innovation.aspx#axzz2EER3eEAB

Index

The following companies where mentioned or used as cases to illustrate and strengthen certain principles and concepts (alphabetical listing):

Ambient Devices
http://www.ambientdevices.com

American Express Global
https://www.americanexpress.com/

Apple
http://investor.apple.com

Caesar's
http://www.caesars.com

Mark Cuban
http://markcubancompanies.com/

Digital Equipment Corporation/HP
http://www8.hp.com/us/en/hp-information/index.html

eBay
http://www.ebayinc.com/

European Organization for Nuclear Research (CERN)
http://home.web.cern.ch/

Facebook
http://investor.fb.com/

Fairchild Semiconductor
http://www.fairchildsemi.com/company/

FedEx
http://about.van.fedex.com/fedex_corporation

Google
http://www.google.com/about/company/

Harrah's Entertainment
http://www.harrahsresort.com

IDEO
http://www.ideo.com/

Instagram
http://instagram.com/

iTunes
http://www.itunes.com

Kraft Foods
http://www.kraftfoodsgroup.com/home/index.aspx

Large Hadron Collider (LHC)
http://www.lhc.ac.uk/

LL Bean
http://www.llbean.com

Loylogic
http://www.loylogic.com

MIT Media Lab
http://www.media.mit.edu

Netflix
http://ir.netflix.com

PIXAR
http://www.pixar.com

PointsPay
http://www.pointspay.com

Quickster/Netflix
http://ir.netflix.com/management.cfm

Tinbu
http://www.tinbu.com

YouTube
http://www.youtube.com/t/contact_us

TripAdvisor
http://www.tripadvisor.com/pages/about_us.html

Total Rewards
http://www.totalrewards.com

Volunteers of America
http://www.voa.org

Volunteers of America Northern New England
http://www.voanne.org/

Wyndham Hotel Group
http://www.wyndham.com

Wyndham Rewards
https://www.wyndhamrewards.com

Yahoo
http://info.yahoo.com

About the Author

Brian W. Bickford is an energetic, global technology professional who draws a wealth of insight from 25 years of technology and business process experience, leading international teams through product and business development.

He is a U.S. Air Force veteran and holds an MBA and MS ISM degrees with executive leadership training at MIT. He puts value in continuous professional development, societal contribution, and socially responsible leadership.

At the heart of Brian's philosophy is a strong advocacy for getting the best out of people and mentoring and guidance for business leaders today and tomorrow, through shared wisdom and proven processes that fit in today's world. He is passionate about providing the best navigation and practical advice to help companies succeed and innovators express themselves. Brian is an interactive technology industry expert, successful entrepreneur, executive consultant, and public speaker. He draws inspirations from seeing innovators innovate, creators create, and leaders lead.

www.ingramcontent.com/pod-product-compliance
Lightning Source LLC
Chambersburg PA
CBHW071408170526
45165CB00001B/210